FEEDBACK
DECODED

NEELACANTAN B

INDIA • SINGAPORE • MALAYSIA

Notion Press Media Pvt Ltd

No. 50, Chettiyar Agaram Main Road,
Vanagaram, Chennai, Tamil Nadu – 600 095

First Published by Notion Press 2021
Copyright © Neelacantan B 2021
All Rights Reserved.

ISBN 978-1-63850-591-4

This book has been published with all efforts taken to make the material error-free after the consent of the author. However, the author and the publisher do not assume and hereby disclaim any liability to any party for any loss, damage, or disruption caused by errors or omissions, whether such errors or omissions result from negligence, accident, or any other cause.

While every effort has been made to avoid any mistake or omission, this publication is being sold on the condition and understanding that neither the author nor the publishers or printers would be liable in any manner to any person by reason of any mistake or omission in this publication or for any action taken or omitted to be taken or advice rendered or accepted on the basis of this work. For any defect in printing or binding the publishers will be liable only to replace the defective copy by another copy of this work then available.

Contents

Foreword   5

Acknowledgements   7

Preface   11

Introduction   15

The Trigger   17

Chapter 1   What is Feedback?   23

Chapter 2   Feedback is Omnipresent   38

Chapter 3   What does Good Feedback Look Like?   45

Chapter 4   The Inner Workings of Feedback Frameworks   51

Chapter 5   And yet, Why is it Difficult to give Feedback?   58

Chapter 6   The Art of Feedback in Various Situations   68

Chapter 7   Step in: Create a Culture of Feedback in Your Team   77

Chapter 8	The Ultimate Conversation Framework	90
Chapter 9	The Counter-Intuitive Way	112
Chapter 10	What about Difficult Conversations?	132
Chapter 11	Use Questions to get Better at Feedback	145
Chapter 12	The Receiver is Equally Afraid	153
Chapter 13	Making Feedback Work for You	157
Chapter 14	Feedback as the Ultimate Leverage for All Competencies	172

Rounding off	*181*
Feedback Decoded	*183*
Detailed Examples	*193*
Bonus – On Written Feedback	*201*
Appendix	*209*
Notes and References	*217*

Foreword

Feedback—the word evokes a memory for each one of us and usually it's a negative one – of hearing what we did not do well or what was not liked. If you ask leaders and managers, what has been the most difficult professional conversation of their lives – over 90% are bound to say "feedback" in some shape or form.

Feedback is often seen as a negative and sporadic event that occurs between two people, usually addressing an immediate or short term event. And a difficult conversation to somehow be gotten over with.

Imagine a business world where Feedback evokes positive memories and where managers and leaders regard it as an impactful and meaningful conversation. Imagine the possibilities of growth and enrichment that it could offer.

This book demystifies Feedback and gives it centre stage as the "crux of all skills". A skill that enables positive and open relationships, clarifies expectations, encourages transparency, enhancing two-way communication and delivers growth apart from enabling the building of almost all leadership competencies.

Neel simplifies the feedback journey – breaking its traditional mould of being a lengthy engagement that is emotionally loaded. The simple steps and templates make feedback an easy process that is not cognitively loaded – making it accessible to young managers, startup founders and entrepreneurs.

– Radhika Bhalla, Organization Psychologist

Acknowledgements

Writing a book has been a long pending dream – though I must admit that writing a book on Feedback did not occur to me in the wildest of my dreams.

I started writing this book around the time when the pandemic struck. I thought this was a good way to make productive use of my time. I wrote about 35,000 words, which, as difficult as it was, seemed easy when I started work on the editing. So, thanks to my family for having borne my writing and editing routine. Without their giving space and being patient, this would never have happened.

Behind every successful book is a hustle. Thanks to Koushik for creating the hustle in me to make it happen. Without his impetus, my book project was a slow moving train towards nowhere. He gave a destination, a timeline and the motivation (provocation?) to make it happen. He made it worse by inquiring about the progress periodically as well. Thank you, Aparna Chandrasekhar, for patiently sitting through the many virtual editing sessions, writing comments on the Google Doc and patiently and gently reviewing them, highlighting them and sharing your inputs. Thank you, Charusmitha Rao, among other things, for making me rethink the title to what it is, and Vijayalakshmi Chari and Yamini Koganti, for having read bits and pieces and suggested edits. Thanks, Geetha Ramakrishnan, for being detail oriented as usual while reviewing the entire manuscript at one go – my heartfelt gratitude for looking at every line with a fine-toothed comb. Thanks, Radhika Bhalla, for reading the whole manuscript and coming in with fantastic suggestions through the process and of course for having written a wonderful Foreword. Thanks, Sirisha Bhamidipati, for reading the whole manuscript and reassuring me that the flow was good. Thanks to Harsh Pandya for the cover design, the creative illustrations and the quick turnaround time. Thanks to Kaustubh Deshpande, for being the sounding board you always are. And last but not the least, thank you, Balaji Govindarajan, for being an inspirational leader who was instrumental in my move to the Learning and Development side of the world.

Thank you, my clients, for the opportunity for running Feedback (and other) workshops for you. A big thanks to all the participants of the workshops that I have conducted over the years. Thank you for being incredibly participative and asking questions that have all found their way into this book.

Thank you, readers, for the encouragement by buying the book in digital or physical form and sharing feedback. And thanks, Notion Press, for being encouraging and supportive in this journey.

Neelacantan B (Neel)

Bangalore

2021

Note: The situations mentioned in the book are true situations suitably modified, combined, adapted in a way that they can be used as examples. No names are used. The initials are random.

Preface

It was by sheer serendipity that the topic of Feedback became an area of expertise in my life. I was head of the Learning Function in different capacities at three companies at various points in time. Some years before the first time I became a Talent Development head, I was part of the HR + Business team that had to roll out the dreaded Feedback session just before appraisal season – which was every six months. The content of this course was inadequate, to say the least, and it was repeated at least 10 times in my 7-year career there till then. Among other things, it had a grainy video that was likely created when video was invented. It was outdated and disconnected with the issues on the ground when it came to feedback, but mostly people did not notice it since they slept through the mandatory session. Given a choice, people would prefer to be tortured than sit in this session. But since the company took training very seriously and we had attendance trackers flying around on mail, we sat in those workshops like ancient slaves chained to the seats to row the galley, played shoot the breeze, got those checkboxes ticked, the smiley sheets signed and appraisal conversations continued merrily southward. And, Learning and Development (LnD) met their goals.

And when I became talent development head, the first thing I did was request permission from my manager to junk this module. He said, why don't we start from scratch? I worked with my manager (Balaji Govindarajan, thank you) to create a session on Feedback. It took me a few weeks and a few iterations to put it together as a workshop. I was apprehensive. We picked a new business unit leader who had asked for a Feedback workshop for his leadership team. It helped that he had no previous history of the earlier Feedback session. This session, surprisingly for me and my manager (more me than him – he was unflappable as usual), was a hit. I still remember the first workshop that we conducted which I facilitated. People sat in the room for 8 hours straight without taking any phone calls, actively participated in discussions and role plays and went back energized. The session was a huge success. The word spread. And other leaders began to ask for it.

From running away from Feedback workshops, teams began to request more of it. After the appraisal season, which was my last there, we all forgot about it, went our different ways. I moved companies and eventually started a small independent consulting practice – Outthinc Consulting – at the intersection of Business Learning and Innovation in 2016.

As I pondered around where I should start, I looked at things at the intersection of my large range of interests, small area of expertise, gaps in the market and an even longer list of things I did not want to do. The obvious answer was "Feedback" – mostly because the market saw it differently and I had an idea of how to run a good workshop on Feedback. And it seemed to be something the company needed. It was an instance of "Ikigai" I thought.

Thus, the first content pack that I decided to create was on "Feedback."

As I conducted multiple workshops, I realized that there were many elements of giving and receiving feedback that were not covered elsewhere.

That there was a need for feedback and that it was also one of the core skills that a manager needs to build dawned upon me over time. That this was one of the underrated and neglected building blocks for managerial skills was evident as well.

This book is a ready reckoner regardless of which side of the feedback table you are on. Or your level or your tenure. Whether you are a founder of a startup or the head of a firm or a manager leading your own team. Simply because feedback is such a universal skill worth getting better at. And yes, even if you know everything about feedback, I believe and hope you will find value in the book or recommend it to someone who might benefit.

What you will read in the following pages is a deep dive into the practical mechanics of giving and receiving feedback. You will also be able to connect this to the larger picture of managerial and leadership conversations. You will learn about some myths that have lasted longer than they should. There are indeed many books written on feedback, but two things stand out – one, a practical Indian management perspective and, two, answers to questions that we have on feedback but did not know whom to ask. I have also included a range of situations that I hope will be useful to you as you deepen your skill in giving and receiving feedback.

You will also discover that feedback is one basic skill that, if every manager in the organization upskills on, will enable the organization much more than any other <insert favourite buzzword>. This is because feedback is the foundational element of getting culture right. Also in an age where companies are doing away with ratings, continuous conversations and dialogues (aka feedback) are required to ensure the success of new performance evaluation methods.

I hope that this book and the accompanying frameworks result in good conversations and even better feedback conversations. Thank you for reading.

Introduction

The topic feedback needs no introduction – because we know it either by its absence (I never get feedback) or by its unruly presence (I hate these feedback sessions). However, much of the issue with feedback is a skill issue which, if people and companies cared enough, can be put to very good use. The goal of this book is to simplify this for you. Throughout the book a cast of characters stays with you to make it easy to follow the cases.

This book is for you if you are expected to give feedback to your reportee, peer or boss regardless of whether your title is a manager or not. If you are a leader, a startup founder or an entrepreneur running your own venture – you will find it useful in your day-to-day work. The examples are largely corporate based but the questions and situations are common across. The aim of the book is to simplify Feedback giving and receiving and to connect it to the larger set of leadership competencies.

We start off with asking you a Trigger question and getting into understanding what is feedback in Chapter 1. Chapter 2 is about the omnipresent nature of Feedback – even no feedback is feedback. Chapter 3 deconstructs what good feedback looks like. Chapter 4 is the first and most simple framework of feedback you can deploy. Fears of feedback are dealt with in Chapter 5. Chapter 6 is the Art of Feedback in various situations with many role plays and additional frameworks. Chapter 7 tackles how to create a culture of feedback by Stepping in. Chapter 8 introduces the ultimate conversation framework – a framework that can be deployed for any conversation. Chapter 9 introduces appreciation as a powerful method of feedback. Difficult conversations are tackled in Chapter 10. Chapter 11 tackles the usage of questions as part of feedback conversations. Chapter 12 gives a glimpse into the feedback receiver's mind. Understand how to make feedback work for you in your roles in Chapter 13. And finally, in Chapter 14, we discuss how Feedback is the game changer in building all your leadership competencies.

Happy Reading

The Trigger

Your manager wants an urgent meeting with you!

What goes on in your mind? What is your first reaction?

Pause and think about this for a minute before you read further.

I have asked this question to hundreds of people across many companies in India. Companies across the spectrum – Electronics and Telecommunication, Technology companies, Product companies, Pharmaceutical companies, Consumer Durables. The answer unanimously remains the same.

Take a guess?

The responses are along these lines:

Something has gone wrong!

What did I do?

Something bad has happened.

Oh my god …

Quick let me find out if all is well …

Oh no, not again!

Note: There is a 5% who say something different, "I don't know" or "I would be curious" or "I look forward to hearing from the manager."

In two situations people responded with "I look forward." The first was a company where the culture was "manager as a coach" and the second was an individual who was able to drive a culture of transparency in his team.

Once, the head of the team, who was also in the room, was shocked when the answers all around were along these lines. And he said, "I never thought I was like that." And the reaction is not surprising at all. It is a blind spot! We are blissfully unaware of the massive effect this behaviour of ours has on the team around us.

There are two things here. One, that as a company you can have a culture of feedback that is non-threatening and well-meaning to help the individual. The second is that regardless of company culture, you can instil a culture of feedback within your team. You can create a habit of conversation and dialogue.

Now, answer this question:

At work, what percentage of the feedback you get is appreciative and what percentage is critical?

When I say critical, I also include negative feedback, developmental feedback, well-meaning feedback intended for the good of the person or work or organization, judgemental and non-judgemental feedback, areas of improvement feedback or feedback delivered poorly in a way that you feel upset – pretty much everything that is not appreciation.

The most common answer in the room – starts at 70% (appreciative) and 30% (critical) and soon settles at a politically correct 50–50 and then sheepishly, the room moves to 30% (appreciative) and 70% (critical). I am inclined to believe the 30%–70% figure at junior levels. At senior levels, appreciation is still lower, but negative feedback could also be lower (why is that so?)

Why is it that the unanimous responses to these questions are negative?

And how is this connected to Feedback?

The response to the question in your mind is "cued" – the more your manager has called you for an urgent meeting and used it to convey displeasure – the more likely it is that you will expect it to happen the next time you are called. That is the vicious and virtuous circle of feedback.

The vicious cycle of feedback

The virtuous circle of feedback.

Overall, one tends to receive lesser appreciative feedback. Most feedback you receive is negative or critical feedback – hence when you are called for an urgent meeting, you don't expect to be appreciated.

PS: When the manager question is flipped to, "What percentage of feedback that you give to your team is 'critical' and what percentage is 'appreciative' – people give themselves higher scores than they give their managers." There is nothing surprising about that – it is a blind spot.

Note: All of these are anecdotal, based on what people shared in my workshops. I was unable to find definitive research that supports this, though broadly people agree with the points stated.

Chapter 1

What is Feedback?

The Cast:

Vani: The boss

Manoj: Manager

Ashwin, Dheeraj: Manoj's team

Picture an incident from your childhood where you said something wrong to someone in school, or got miserable scores in an exam, or knocked over the neighbour's bicycle, with the neighbour on it, or broke a window during a game of cricket and ran away. And your parents want to "talk" to you. This is our earliest exposure to feedback – and it is usually not a pleasant experience.

So, let's begin at the start. What is Feedback at work? Beyond the technical definition, feedback is the ability to have candid conversations in the context of work to your superior, manager, subordinate or peer.

Therefore,

Feedback is a skill that can be learnt.

To say – It is a conversation.

Candid conversations – Candid means you are able to state what you feel about a particular situation without judgement. It also means there is no need to withhold information or data.

Across levels Feedback is feedback regardless of level or position.

What is missing in the above definition is that this has to be a regular and a two-way process.

And have the conversation. And that takes a little bit of courage – to talk rather than hold back, ignore it, save it for later (by which time it has become more difficult or the time has passed) or take the path of least resistance and do nothing.

Does it sound complicated? It isn't.

The first issue in giving feedback is not the giving itself – it is the ability to say it in a way that the feedback is received well. Many of us do convey feedback – it is just that we don't give feedback to the person who is supposed to receive it or we convey it in a manner that the other person does not receive it.

In the absence of a model, here is how we do it (and mistake it to be feedback).

1. Peer or upward feedback

    a. Make it a water cooler conversation

    b. Talk to others about it hoping it somehow reaches the intended person

c. Nowadays – post on glassdoor, if it is too much to handle, especially after one has quit the company and is no longer hampered by the fear of consequences. (And besides we are saving others who are stuck in that "hellhole" by posting this.)

d. Lash out when it becomes too much to handle

e. Post on social media – anonymously

f. Scream in rage

g. Spread rumours

2. Reportees

a. Talk incoherently and ramble on and on

b. Avoid/ignore

c. Go on silent mode

d. Pretend all is well

e. Give leadership speeches

f. And the opposite of (e), bury your head under the sand and pretend all is well

3. Other methods

a. Go home and sleep

b. Hit the bar

c. Take the frustration out on somebody else (sometimes the hapless recipients are family, pets, traffic and restaurant waiters)

d. Change the Display Picture on the phone as a subliminal message to the boss, who might click on it and see the message and interpret it as a message for him, and expect him to mend ways.

   e. Eat

   f. Workout

3. <Insert your own passive aggressive method>

   These above methods often make the feedback giver feel better momentarily, but they don't help resolve the underlying issue. Even if the lashing out or the screaming in rage happens, the feedback receiver is at a loss as to what exactly went wrong and what is the remedial action the person is supposed to take. And more often than not, it impacts the image/reputation of the person who lashed out ("immature").

Feedback as a Feedback on Our Culture

Many years ago in college, I had a small job I had taken up during a vacation. This job was a door-to-door survey job. The survey we did was to take feedback on a "moisturizer." I was in the third year of college at the time. And my mentor was a person who was not very well educated but a master in his field. He would analyze which doorbell to ring and what to say for different names on the nameplate. He had his own code for behaving with different ethnicities of Indians – most of which worked.

During our very first survey briefing, he told us, "When you have given a sample (the moisturizer), people will not tell you anything bad. They will tell you everything is good. The product is fantastic. I loved it. But finally you launch the product – nobody will buy it.

This is a bit of an Indian trait. We are not great focused conversationalists. Neither are we direct – when we have to say something. We tend to beat around the bush and give vague responses.[1]

We are also largely hierarchical, so giving feedback to superiors is not easy. Anecdotally, we tend to avoid even mildly difficult conversations. We are great to converse with on general terms, but we back out when it comes to discussing real issues. We may even blow our top off in anger and shout – but that does little to enhance our

> conversation skills. There is a cultural aspect to this,[2] though this is changing as more and more companies and cultures operate out of India.

Consider the Situation.

Manoj has to give feedback to Ashwin, who walks in late into the meeting. How would Manoj respond to Ashwin?

Typical responses would range from – and some of these are very Indian approaches:

Direct: "Why are you late?" or "You were late" to "Can't you be on time?"

Neither here nor there: Making any other sarcastic comments usually coming from a position of authority.

Indirect: At other times managers use their relationship to give the message "on the side" without resorting to direct conversation.

Notice that almost none of this helps, nor is it feedback (though in the unskilled feedback giver's mind, it is meant to be taken as feedback) and it rarely results in a behaviour change (surprise, surprise).

Now let's see the most fundamental and still possibly the most useful model for Feedback – a simple model with high value.

The first model is the SBI model which stands for Situation, Behaviour, Impact. Created by The Centre for Creative Leadership, it is a simple model that is easy to understand and practice.[3]

SBI stands for:

Situation: State the situation or context.

Behaviour: What was the observed behaviour?

Impact: What was the result of it? What was its impact?

What would the feedback look like if Manoj used the SBI model?

Situation: *Hey Ashwin, we were supposed to start at 10.*

Behaviour: *And you came in 10 minutes late.*

Impact: *We could not cover the topics we had intended to and you were the lead presenter. I was counting on you to make a good impression.*

There can be more than one impact as you see below (Impact 2)

Possible Impact 1: *As someone who is expected to lead the team, it creates a poor impression on the team.*

Possible Impact 2: *In a 30-minute meeting, 10 minutes is a big deal. The client could think that we don't care.*

What might Ashwin say?

Yes, sorry Manoj, I had a punctured tyre; so to fix it and come took a few minutes. I drove fast but I could still only manage to reach 10 min late.

How could Manoj respond to that?

> Manoj, Sure. I did not know that – you could have informed me, we would have been prepared.

Sorry, Manoj – I had a slight emergency and had to rush to the doctor in the morning. That's why I was delayed.

How will you respond as Manoj?

> Manoj, Oh is it, take care. You could have informed beforehand; we would have been prepared and you could have taken time out.
>
> *Yes, Manoj, I did not want to do that – I did not want to miss this meeting.*
>
> Manoj, Thanks for your dedication Ashwin, but next time do sound me out in case something comes up.

Is this feedback really necessary could be a question that crosses your mind?

Yes

Is this micromanagement?

No, it isn't.

Ashwin, "Thanks Manoj. I am sorry that I put the team through this today. It was a genuine miss on my part. I will take care of it in future."

Manoj sat back and smiled. He recalled how when he had joined this company, he was a non-believer in the concept of Feedback. He told Vani in his first 1:1 when he had joined 4 years ago, *"Vani, I am not sure. Do we need feedback at all? Admittedly, a lot of feedback is useless to the receiver. The giver gives feedback because he or she has to. Sometimes superficial observations, tangential points coming from the biases of the feedback giver and sheer judgement passes off as feedback. I have not had a great experience with this process. So, I don't believe in it."*

Vani, "Yes, I hear you. Would you like to work with me in trying out the Feedback-led model of managing your team? If it doesn't work, you can switch to your method. But give this a try for 6 months. What do you think?"

"I am a sceptic, Vani. We are all adults here. Everybody is doing their best and nobody needs to be chaperoned. So, if we all agree to that, we can work splendidly well."

Vani said nothing. Manoj noted her demeanour was unlike the previous managers he had worked with. This pause was making him uncomfortable.

Finally, after what seemed to be a long time she spoke, "So, Manoj, are you aware of the Johari Window?"

"Have heard of it. It is an HR concept that they share every now and then in trainings."

"And?"

"And nothing. That's all," Manoj said with a smile.

"So, tell me how have you uncovered your blind spots in your career, Manoj?"

"In my previous job, my boss usually told me and I worked from there."

"Tell me more."

Manoj was a little irritated at this point, but he continued …

"Well no, it is more complicated than that, but mostly he would forget the feedback or I would ignore what was said and continue or I would just continue to do what I felt was right. Or I might go ahead and do something to prove the feedback wrong."

"So what I hear you say is that your boss's feedback was a one-way communication?"

"Yes," said Manoj, shrugging his shoulders. "Isn't that always the case?"

Vani smiled. "Maybe there is a better way," she finally said after a long pause.

"So, Manoj," she continued, "tell me one thing, How does your team know how well they are performing? If *you want the team to get to higher performance levels, how do you get them there?"*

"Status reports. Work reviews. Isn't it visible to us at all times?"

"Yes, but is that enough?"

"It has been enough so far."

Vani sensed a bit of impatience and did not want to drag the conversation.

"So, in the interest of time, how about giving 'feedback-led team management' a try?"

"Sure," said Manoj, not wanting to disagree with the boss in the very first meeting and wondered if he had sounded too candid. Anyway he believed that these were just new initiatives that every boss promises – and they will be the first to be swept away under the carpet when a new deliverable looms.

However, Vani seemed to walk the talk. She was very particular about her one-on-one meetings with Manoj. She let him lead the conversation every time and listened well. When it was her turn, she seemed to be well prepared. She recalled specific context, explicitly stated the observed behaviour (of Manoj) and the impact it had. For instance she said, *"Manoj, in the last brainstorming meeting, you shot down Dheeraj's ideas both the times. He was silent for most parts of the meeting later on and hardly spoke. This typically discourages team members from speaking up; how about getting everyone's ideas up, engaging them in explaining it further and collectively doing a poll to pick what looks more promising?"*

The johari window is a depiction of what parts of ourselves we know and what are known to others. That is depicted in a 2X2 matrix here.

There are aspects of our behaviour that are known to others and unknown to us. This is what constitutes the blind spot in the Johari Window. If we do not seek feedback, our blind spots will not be uncovered. Therefore feedback is essential for our own growth.

> A common blind spot is interrupting someone while they are speaking.
>
> Blind spots may also be positive. At the end of a panel discussion in college, the professor asked the class for feedback. And one student said, "Whenever Neel is on the panel, he comes up with something creative." That was the first time I had even thought of myself as creative. It was a blind spot.
>
> Giving and receiving feedback is a proven method of uncovering one another's blind spots.

So is feedback all that it promises to be? Yes – all it needs is a level of awareness and skill. And note that a one-off feedback will not accomplish much, but sustained feedback and follow-up will.

Often we tend to construe feedback only as negative or corrective feedback. Giving appreciative feedback is actually the bigger, more underrated part of the feedback process. But how can one seek feedback and use it to improve one's own understanding of self?

> Indeed "Good job" is the worst feedback one can get. It does not tell you what was good (someone liked it? Someone slogged? Customer got something on time? My algorithm was good? Boss in a good mood?) or what was repeatable (should I slog? Should I spend long hours in the office? Should I slog for someone's poor planning?) and what was learnt in this experience (how to take this to the next level).
>
> How would "Good job" sound when delivered well?
>
> Here is Manoj sharing feedback to Ashwin on something that has gone well.
>
> Situation: *In the current customer escalation*
>
> Behaviour: *You led from the front, ensuring that our eyes were on the goal and took responsibility beyond your role.*
>
> Impact: *With the result, we closed it in good time within SLA.*
>
> And when you appreciate using the SBI format, you enable a person to see the learning moment within what went well.

Try the SBI method at home or at the office, with kids or grown-ups, for appreciation or improvement. The results will surprise you.

> *Do we need to share feedback every time someone comes late? Isn't that trivial?*
>
> *If the "coming late" had an impact then that feedback has to be shared. At that point not sharing the feedback is a lack of "managerial courage" to call out dysfunctional behaviour as it happens (what is referred to as "in the moment feedback"). That in essence is real-time feedback.*
>
> *If the "coming late" has no impact, there is no need to share the feedback.*

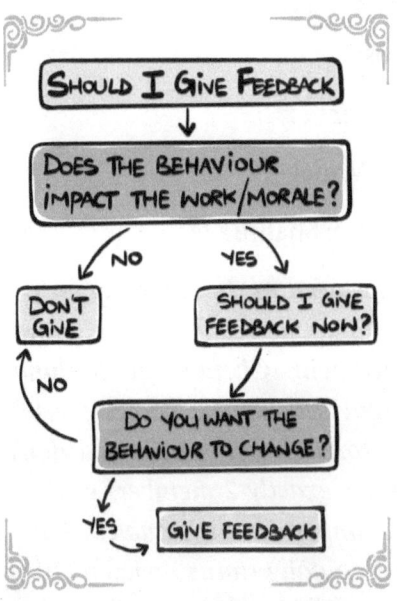

TLDR: Whenever you are in a position to give feedback try using the Situation Behaviour Impact (SBI) framework in situations positive and negative. Make this into a habit with deliberate practice.

Chapter 2

Feedback is Omnipresent

The Cast:

Vani: The boss

Manoj: Manager

Shalini: New Manager

Chetan, Sushma: Shalini's team

Shalini has been in the company for 6 months now. She meets Manoj for coffee. "You know, I am kind of exasperated with Chetan and Sushma. Sushma is headstrong and believes she knows everything. Chetan doesn't want to work with Sushma. I don't know what to do. There are exactly 2 members in the team and we are up for an important deliverable. I have shared their goals and we do daily status reviews. Other than that I have refused to fall into their trap of disliking each other. Each day they fight like siblings."

"And what do you think is happening to the team with this approach?"

"They will realize that I am not interested in their rivalry and focus on the goals. And having conversations with them on anything else other than goals is a waste of time. So I have stopped giving them any feedback for now. Vani is not going to like it."

"It may be worth a conversation with Vani, you know."

"You think so?" she said reluctantly. *"I will set up time in that case."*

Shalini met Vani the following day

"Hi Shalini, how are things?"

Shalini needed only a hint to pour her heart out.

Vani smiled. Her constant smile irritated Shalini, but what she said after that seemed worth it.

"Shalini, have you noticed that feedback is 'ever present' even when one does not receive it? Think about it. If I don't receive any feedback from my manager, it is still feedback – Feedback that the manager doesn't care, doesn't know, doesn't think it is important enough. These are extreme reactions, but at a fundamental level, the team member probably feels that it is not worth being given feedback on due to a variety of reasons (legitimate or otherwise). So, what do you think your team is thinking?"

"That the manager is not interested?"

"Maybe."

"Or couldn't care less."

"Possible."

"So, it looks like I have to talk to the team. Oh, this is so stressful."

Lack of feedback is feedback too. A Gallup report states that employees would rather receive negative feedback than no feedback at all.[4]

Anecdotally, feedback from the manager drops as the perceived ease of getting work done through the team member reduces. Communication levels drop as discomfort increases.

Temporarily, the issue might appear to be taken care of, but it has created new problems. Someone else is taking on an unfair share of the workload while the other employee is not given the feedback she deserves to be given.

Often when performance dips, we ignore the low performer. This is rationalized – after all, it is not worth the time anyway. But the team is carrying along an unproductive person and the team loses efficiency.

On the other hand, if the assessment was wrong and it we lose the opportunity to groom a good performer for the future. Now this employee will start looking out – first within the company, and very soon outside it.

Assume you are driving from point A to point C and you have someone giving you feedback as you go from point A to point C.

What if along the way your goal was changed to point B and you did not know it?

And what if your year-end performance was measured on how far you are from point B.

> Obviously, you will be surprised – and not particularly happy about it.
>
> If your goal had changed from point B to point C, you should have been told about it at the midway rest/fuel stop so that you could take the appropriate detour.
>
> Like driving requires continuous feedback – eyes on the road, the GPS, the route map and adjustment to ensure you stay on track, on route – so too worklife requires continuous feedback.

Overall, there are 4 types of feedback conversations one might have.

1. Day-to-day feedback – stay on track. Minor adjustments may be required.

2. Things are going well. You may offer additional specific inputs here.

3. Performance feedback (maybe includes a career conversation).

4. Course correction.

Out of the above, "The fear is related to giving only one type of feedback": where you have to give feedback to your team member about a major course correction.

How does feedback change in a remote first environment?

Generally, face to face is the best way to give feedback. Block a mutually agreed time and share the feedback.

In a virtual world, the golden rule is to have a video call. This is the next best thing to a face-to-face meeting. Second, if I had to give a hierarchy, it would be this:

Use WhatsApp (or any chat channel) groups to share feedback in public, or any news like good news, awards, achievements. These don't need a team meeting for sharing.

Follow that up with an email. Mails are good for records.

Repeat the appreciation in the team meeting. Use the meeting to check in on "learning points" based on what went well.

If it is bad news that has to be shared – group issues can be shared in the group only for information. The longer discussion is best held in a closed group meeting. However, when discussing as a group, focus on solutions, come to an agreement on the next steps and close.

Individual feedback conversations have to be delivered in private. Ping on WhatsApp/slack/teams to block time and proceed accordingly.

> There is no change in the models.
>
> Use email to close the loop. Use email for anything that requires both sides to agree. Use email as a means to follow up and as a record.

All said and done, Feedback is a constant process regardless of whether work is done from an office or remote locations.

TLDR: Lack of feedback is also feedback – a feedback to be complacent or taken for granted.

Chapter 3

What does Good Feedback Look Like?

The Cast:

Vani: The boss

Shalini: Manager who is new

Chetan, Sushma: Shalini's team

Shalini meets Vani. "You know, I am kind of exasperated with Chetan and Sushma to say the least. Very little has changed since we spoke last. I do not want to sound helpless here, but these guys have been with the company longer than I have. I am curious to know what to do in this case, how often should I be talking to them?"

Vani sighed, "Yes, Shalini. This may seem counter-intuitive – but the more conversations you have with your team – of any nature – the easier it is to have tough conversations. Lack of regular feedback is often a reason for employee disengagement. Therefore, ask yourself what would it take for you to have regular conversations with the team? Not "hi, how are you" conversations."

Shalini murmured, "You don't have people like Chetan and Sushma in your team."

Vani continued, "Yes, even with Chetan and Sushma regular feedback will work. It will take a bit of time, but it will work."

Shalini dreaded the prospect of having regular conversations with Chetan and Sushma. "I am not sure."

Vani, "Try it, it will work."

This began to sound like management speak. Vani continued, "As their manager, keep conversation lines open via two-way feedback. Make your relationships transparent with your team. Your team needs to know where it stands."

While sharing feedback, remember the overall rule for any feedback is CORBS.[5]

C: Clear

O: Owned

R: Regular

B: Balanced

S: Specific

What does Clear feedback mean?

Clear is the opposite of vague. Clarity is stating the what – Is this working? Is it not? Is it good? Is it bad? Should I change? Should I not? This has to be stated in black-and-white terms.

What does Owned mean?

Owned means that this is your feedback, not someone else's. *Many years ago someone walked up to me at a group offsite and said, "Because of you, I got dinged in the appraisal cycle." I was puzzled. It was at least a year since he had reported to me and I was not responsible for his rating any longer – he reported to someone else. He told me that his manager told him, "Neel felt you aren't contributing to an initiative, hence your rating is lower this time."*

This is familiar – an easy cop out is to tell your reportee, *"I wanted to give you a higher rating, but HR or <Insert favourite scapegoat> did not allow me."*

Even if HR did, ultimately it is your stand, so own your feedback when you share it with your teams.

So, if you hear feedback from your manager, *"Robert told me, your performance needs to improve,"* what should your response be?

> My response would be:
>
> - What do you think?
> - More than Robert, I want to know what you think.
> - What is your opinion?

What does Regular mean?

Regular means timely. That the feedback is given on a timely basis – as close to the event as possible. Also ensure that you use regular 1:1s for sharing feedback.

What does Balanced mean?

Balanced means having a sense of balance while communicating feedback. It is about seeing what can be bettered when the feedback is all "good" and seeing what is good when the feedback is all "negative." The key to balance is being genuine – do not make up something for the sake of balance. Also remember balance is over time – if you are only sharing critical feedback with your team – think about appreciating them. If you are only appreciating your team, what do you need to do to get them to push themselves more?

(**Note:** Balanced feedback is not sandwich feedback)

What is Specific?

Specific is the opposite of general. Your communication skills need to improve is a general feedback. Specific is, *your formal conversation skills need to improve.* The specificity is about the specific behaviour that needs to change or continue or be amplified.

The lack of any one of the elements of CORBS makes the feedback vague.

For instance, the most common words written in performance reviews is "Communication skills needs to improve" is neither clear nor specific or Balanced or Owned or Regular for that matter, which is as vague as it gets.

> Aside: Good job lacks almost all aspects of CORBS. Good job is not Clear (Good job of what?). It is not Owned – though it sounds like it is owned, good job is vague on the ownership. It is not Regular (happens when an event qualified to be good job happens). It is not Balanced (was everything good?) and it is not Specific (exactly what was the goodness). Sure, appreciate by saying, Good Job – but take time to share the details of what made it a good job.

Think of CORBS as the overarching rule for any feedback conversation regardless of model.

TLDR: Clear Owned Regular Balanced Specific (CORBS) is the overarching framework to keep in mind every time you give feedback. Jot down CORBS for the feedback you are supposed to give or received and see what is missing.

Chapter 4

The Inner Workings of Feedback Frameworks

The Cast:

Shalini: Manoj's peer manager who is new

Chetan, Sushma: Shalini's team

Shalini, *"Chetan, I wanted to share some feedback with you?"*

Chetan, *"Is this about me and Sushma?"*

Shalini, *"Well, yes and no."*

Chetan, *"Why don't you share feedback with her?"*

Shalini, *"I will, but first I would want you to listen to me. This constant rivalry between the two of you is driving me up the wall. I feel we are unable to get anything done because of the two of you."*

Chetan, *"Why me? Why are you sharing his feedback only with me? Isn't Sushma to blame as well? All this is because Sushma is a woman and I have no voice."*

Shalini, "This has nothing to do with that."

Chetan, "You joined recently and you have no idea about my contributions to this company."

Shalini, "I am aware of all your contributions."

Chetan, "I have been awarded thrice in the last 12 months – doesn't that count for something? Clearly, I am capable, am I not? So why am I being blamed?"

Shalini, "I want you to hear my perspective."

Chetan, "I am not sure this is important. We are meeting all deliverables. How does it matter? I feel the company doesn't recognize my contribution."

Feedback models + CORBS ensure that digressions such as these can be handled.

Feedback delivered without a model can be perceived wrongly in many ways. In the above example, when Shalini say, *"I will, but first I would want you to listen to me. This constant rivalry of the two of you is making our deliverables delayed."* it comes across as an opinion. *I feel we are unable to get anything done because of the two of you.* Here the person (Chetan) feels that he is being singled out for feedback.

Sometimes, the conversation veers off into uncharted territory. *Chetan, "Why me? Why are you sharing his feedback only with me? Isn't Sushma to blame as well? All this is because Sushma is a woman and I have no voice."*

Or into time. *Chetan, "You joined recently and you have no idea about my contributions to this company."*

Or into behaviour. *Chetan, "I have been awarded thrice in the last 12 months – doesn't that count for something? Clearly, I am capable, am I not? So why am I being blamed?"*

Sometimes the conversation switches to *"So, what? It was no big deal."*

Chetan, "I am not sure this is important. We are meeting all deliverables. How does it matter?"

Tip: One of the good ways to land SBI model–based feedback well is to use "I" statements rather than "you" statements, or "what" instead of "who."

Shalini, "Chetan, May I share some feedback?"

Chetan, "Is this about me and Sushma?"

Shalini, "We can discuss it when we meet. When can we catch up?"

Chetan, "Why don't you share feedback with her?"

Shalini, "Of course! I do plan to."

Chetan, "Ok, let's meet tomorrow at 10:30 am."

The next day

Shalini, "Hi, Chetan, how are things?"

Chetan, "Good, you had feedback."

Shalini, "So here is the situation. We have an important deliverable coming up."

Chetan, "Hmmm"

Shalini, "This constant rivalry between two of my team members is driving me up the wall."

Chetan, "Hmm"

Shalini, "Some bit of competitiveness is good, but I believe if we work closely, we can do really better, both as individuals and as a team."

Chetan, "Why me? Why are you sharing his feedback only with me? Isn't Sushma to blame as well? All this is because Sushma is a woman and I have no voice?"

Shalini, "I intend to talk to Sushma too."

Chetan, "Ok. You joined recently and you have no idea about my contributions to this company."

Shalini, "So, a couple of things. I want to focus on the three specific incidents that have happened in the last week. In each of these incidents, our output has got delayed because the two of you could not come to an agreement. And you are also aware of it."

Chetan, "I am not sure which three incidents you are referring to. Unless you want to make me responsible for every date our team has missed. In which case there are many more."

Shalini, "There were three specific incidents that I shared with you in the morning."

Chetan, "I don't agree with the diagnosis in the mail. Also, you forget that I have been awarded thrice in the last 12 months – doesn't that count for something? Clearly, I am capable, am I not? So why am I being blamed?"

Shalini, "This is only about the specific situation at hand. Are we clear?"

Chetan, "Yes. But I am not sure this is important. We are meeting all deliverables. How does it matter?"

Shalini, "Chetan, there were three issues in the last week because of which our output was delayed. Can we keep the conversation focused on only these three issues?"

Chetan, "Ok. Tell me."

Notice how the model ensures that the conversation stays within the boundary of the Situation, Behaviour and Impact. Each time the conversation veers off, the model ensures that it is brought back to the issue at hand. Also, the model ensures that the feedback keeps the focus on the issue, not the person.

Without the guardrails of SBI, the scope of feedback automatically gets broadened. And a specific feedback (You came late to this meeting) becomes vague (You do not come on time) or becomes a personal attack (You are the reason we start late).

As a feedback giver, do not exaggerate S or B or I. The feedback has to be authentic. If it is not, both the feedback model and your credibility will be impacted.

The greatest impact of SBI (or any model) is when it is given as close as possible to the moment of the behaviour. That's when the "impact" or evidence is fresh – and cannot be countered by a "how" or a "when" or "but that was a different issue" or by various degrees of forgetfulness.

> How would appreciative feedback sound with SBI?
>
> Team, in the last escalation, we identified the root cause soon without any lag. It was good to see you collaborate and rise to the occasion. As a result the client who was worried about shifting to our services is confident that we can handle their account.

TLDR: Feedback models narrow scope conversations into the here and now. Boxing in the conversation to specifics is a great way to make sure that the feedback is specific and actionable for the recipient. Try using the SBI framework for appreciative and critical feedback.

Chapter 5

And yet, Why is it Difficult to give Feedback?

The Cast:

Vani: The boss

Manoj: Manager

Shalini: Manoj's peer manager who is new

Ashwin, Dheeraj: Manoj's team

Chetan, Sushma: Shalini's team

Shalini and Manoj meet over coffee.

Shalini, "Manoj, I tried giving feedback to Chetan."

Manoj, "It did not work?"

Shalini, "Chetan is irrational."

Manoj, "And what about Sushma?"

Shalini, "She can get really angry. And snap."

Manoj, "Hmmm"

Shalini, "This is my worry. It looks like resolving internal issues itself will take away all our time. God knows when we will actually do our own work."

When we think of the situation where we have to give feedback often the first thought that comes to our mind is that the recipient is a difficult person.

Mostly people aren't difficult. However, a lot of times, they are not used to receiving feedback, so some degree of resistance is expected. Also the feedback giver's skills come into question.

There was a person in my team who was appreciated every year though his skill levels were low – a clear case of the manager's blind spot. So, when I showed him the mirror, it did not go well. It took many conversations to enable the person to see his shortcomings. The person wasn't difficult – the feedback was just never delivered to him.

In my experience, Indian managers tend to either withhold or sugarcoat their negative evaluations of their subordinates.[6] Part of the reluctance stems from their concern for the feelings of the other person, partly from their need to preserve their relationship, but a significant part stems from the need to protect themselves from potential hostility that they may have to face.[7]

> In my workshops, when I state that only a small percentage of the team is irrational – I can see participants smile. So, I ask them, what percentage of your team you think is like this? The answer starts with a laugh and after some discussions narrows down in the range of 1–10%.
>
> And when you say, Let's assume, about 1% of your team is irrational? People accept this and then usually a hand goes up … and someone asks, "What if a large percentage of your team is irrational?"
>
> "One, look within and ask yourself, are you the irrational manager while your team is rational? Or,

> two, check your hiring process if you are indeed hiring irrational players instead of A-players."
>
> The reason being, it is highly unlikely that a large number of irrational people will find their way into an organization. Almost every organization is well tuned to eliminate such impurities from the process. But a 1–5% makes it and is successful as well. And they can be handled by regular feedback using a model.
>
> So yes, maybe a fraction of your reportees are irrational, but don't let that fear or lack of skill come in the way of your belief of building your feedback-giving skills.

I start my feedback workshops by asking people to fill out a situation about feedback which they find difficult to handle. As I collated these over the years, I found a clear pattern.

There are 3 different types of difficulties: Fear, Framing and Consequence.

Fear (Pre-Feedback) is a combination of frightfulness and anxiety about a given feedback situation. This happens because you are not sure how the receiver will take it. It could be because of doubts on whether that feedback should be given. It can also be the uncertainty of the right "evidence" to back the feedback.

Framing (During Feedback) is the ability to convey the message in an impactful manner. Here, one is sure about the feedback, but unsure about how to convey it.

Consequence (Post Feedback) is a constant concern about the aftermath of the feedback conversation.

Commonly cited Pre-Feedback issues, "How do I give feedback in this situation"

- Not performing well on the job, projects delayed, no adherence to timelines
- Recurring issues – Quality, SLA misses etc.
- Has a rigid mindset
- Wants promotion every 2 years
- Works well, but does only what is told
- Has a preconceived notion – feedback will always be bad
- How to get tough with someone who is a nice guy but does very little work?

- Person is going through a personal crisis always/sometimes/now
- Person is not performing as expected
- Person is interested only in visibility, not real work

All of the above requires you to set expectations – which most managers don't do. Setting expectations ensures that the ground rules are set for feedback.

The expectation to be set is on the lines of "As a manager, I will regularly share feedback with you on how you are performing. Some of it could be observations, some of it could be patterns, but I will share feedback."

The second gap is the quality of data/evidence. That means, being in touch with the work sufficiently enough to ensure that the feedback has been thoroughly validated. "How to collect data without being perceived as a nosy micromanager?" is an oft-cited excuse. The data problem can be solved by being more connected with the work, being more objective in terms of deliverables and being more observant.

Added to this is the fear of being perceived as a rigid manager, an unskilled manager or getting low scores in an upcoming manager survey. And the mix of all this ensures feedback is not given.

However, the real benefits of having the conversation outweigh the imagined consequences.

Issues in the Framing

You may decide to give feedback, but when you are confronted with resistance or aggression, you may hold back the next time. For instance, when a person cannot accept minor critical feedback, it leads you to wonder, should I hold back critical points?

Framing enables you to cut to the chase and stay on point. Framing is a lot about structuring the conversation. And here is where Feedback models come in. While framing, do not hold back critical points. And have the conversation with credible data on hand.

Follow up on the Consequence

Almost always, follow-up is about having another conversation, and possibly more conversations after that. Relentless follow-up is a must for adherence to commitments made post feedback. The amount of follow-up can be dialled up or down based on the individual propensity to stick to the commitments. A lot of times people expect that one conversation will set it all right. Conversations followed by commitment, timelines, regular review is what will ensure a genuine behaviour change.

Therefore, how to remedy these fears?

1. Can you say objectively that the person is not performing up to the mark? Have the goals been set well? Are they reviewed

objectively? Does the person know where there are performance gaps? These need to be communicated and reviewed on a regular basis.

2. Almost all pre-feedback issues are about reputation. Either the person comes with a "reputation" based on previous conversations or has been labelled difficult based on one conversation. In most cases this will point back to a skill/data gap (on the part of the feedback giver).

Managerial courage as a competency

1. There is an element of courage that it takes to face the issue head on. Facing these kinds of issues is part of one's own leadership development journey.

2. Very often, if the data is right, managerial courage may not be an issue. Therefore, fix the data first and convince yourself.

3. Practice the small things

    a. Doing the right thing – giving critical feedback when necessary

    b. Appreciate so that reportee doesn't hear only critical feedback

4. It is vital to build one's ability to handle tough conversations with (some degree of) equanimity.

5. For all of this the answer is more practice of feedback conversations, not less

6. Don't wait too long to give feedback. The time to give an issue-based feedback passes by and the issue itself remains unresolved. My own experience is that delayed feedback snowballs and comes back to bite you when you least expect it.

In the book *Thanks for the Feedback* the authors break down the types of conversations as Appreciation, Coaching and Evaluation.[8]

My own preference is to look at conversations through a different lens – easy to difficult in terms of the practicality of giving feedback. Viewed from this perspective, there are 3 basic types of feedback, Day-to-day feedback – which is usually goal focused and is about minor adjustments to ensure work is on track. Then there is appreciation – about a job well done. These two are easy – both to give and receive. The course correction conversation petrifies managers the most. However, if you give sufficient day-to-day feedback and appreciative feedback – the third one is not that difficult. Also day-to-day feedback and appreciation can take a huge chunk of the feedback pie, so what is left is a smaller piece. But because we don't do enough of the others, this suddenly feels more daunting.

I prefer to classify other conversations as – Career conversation, Performance Coaching, Development, Compensation. And in each of them there is an evaluation component that is difficult for the feedback giver. So, the key is to acknowledge the degrees of difficulty in communicating and conveying (and in some cases, the self-realization) of the "difficult" aspect of the conversation.

Try this: Maintain a log of the types of feedback you give to your team. Classify it as per the above – day to day, appreciation and course correction. See if you bring up the sum total of appreciation plus day-to-day feedback to a much higher level than course correction. Warning, it will be difficult and your team will find it odd if you start doing it all of a sudden – but it is worth it.

TLDR: It is common to have fears about giving feedback. Know that there are three types of fears – Fears, Framing and Consequence. Each of them can be dealt with in a different manner.

Most of our fears of giving feedback boil down to two things: an irrational fear of the irrational employee or a doubt that "Am I right about this one?" The first one is a skill-driven question that can be taken care of by the feedback model. The second is all about being sure – so share your feedback as a feedback or an observation. But let these fears not hold you back from the feedback itself. What are your fears?

Chapter 6

The Art of Feedback in Various Situations

The Cast:

Vani: The boss

Manoj: Manager

Shalini: Manoj's peer manager who is new

Ashwin, Dheeraj: Manoj's team

Chetan, Sushma: Shalini's team

On the road to getting better at feedback, I recommend you start with using SBI in Positive feedback situations. Initially, this will seem to be difficult, like with all behaviour changes. Once you get used to it, move to giving all feedback in SBI mode.

How to make SBI better? Here is an approach that I call "SBI plus."

Modify SBI by seeking permission at the outset. Follow it up with SBI and close it with a question or suggestion.

"Can I give you some feedback?" is a good question to start with.

Why ask permission? You don't mean to take no for an answer – so isn't this permission a sham? No.

By asking permission, what you are doing is

- Respecting the individual's time
- Giving them time to be ready
- And giving them a choice on when they want to hear it

If they say, no – honour the no. However, your follow-up question will be, "Sure, when can we meet?" The intent of asking permission is to ensure that you have the conversation at a time of mutual convenience.

You can also frontload the SBI feedback model with a question, "What do you think about the 'Situation' yesterday?"

Close it with a "Good, continue" or "Here is how you can make it better."

You can wrap this with a question as well.

What do you think you can do about it?

How do you think this can be overcome?

How can we make it better?

Question: "*Chetan, can I give you some feedback?*"

"*Sure*"

Shalini, "So here is the situation. We have an important deliverable coming up."

Chetan, "Hmmm"

Shalini, "Wanted to share a concern with you. I noticed in the last few weeks that there is an unstated competition between you and Sushma."

Chetan, "Hmm yes. Both of us want to do better."

Shalini, "Some bit of competitiveness is good, but I believe if we work closely, we can do really better, both for you as a person and for us as a team. Currently, the way I see it, it is a little more than competition – probably an interest in bringing each other down."

Chetan, "Yes, it may have happened. Will take care of it."

Shalini, "In the past I have allowed both of you to sort things out, but now I feel this has come to a head and I am looking at a weekly review with both of you."

Chetan, "I am not convinced it is so severe."

Shalini, "Possible, but this quarterly deliverable is not something I can risk given that we slipped in last week's milestone with a fairly major bug that was preventable given both your expertise. If information was shared in advance, this would not have happened is the way I see it."

Chetan, "Ok."

Shalini, "I want to know from you (and her) how we can ensure that your competitiveness does not come in the way of our deliverables, or even better, if we can use your competitiveness for the greater good of the team. I will leave you with this thought."

Chetan, "Sure, Thanks."

Shalini, "Thanks."

Once you are comfortable giving SBI (or SBI plus) feedback, the next step is to give pattern-based feedback.

Often managers wait to see a pattern before giving a pattern-based feedback; whereas the fact is that the more issue-based feedback you give the easier it becomes to give pattern feedback.

What if I am not sure if it is a pattern or not? What if I am not sure if it warrants a feedback or not?

I have seen leaders tackle both of these questions in similar ways.

Approach 1

Manoj, "Ashwin, can I share an observation with you?"

Ashwin, "Sure."

Manoj, "There are situations where you appear to be helpless. Or pretend that you do not have the authority to deal with something."

Ashwin, "Hmm ... I am not sure I see it that way."

Manoj, "Fair enough. What I want you to know is that you have the authority and I want you to exercise that authority instead of feeling helpless."

Approach 2

Manoj, "Ashwin, can I share some feedback?"

Ashwin, "Sure."

Manoj, "Here is something I noticed. This is not a pattern, but I think it is worth bringing to your notice. In the last two meetings with the leadership team, there have been situations where you have been unable to convince the team on the stand you took. This might come from two positions – either you have genuinely changed your point of view or you were unsure of your stand at the start. So, what would you like to do about that?"

Ashwin, "I never thought about it that way. I always thought I was being flexible and taking views into account. Never realized it comes across like that. Let me mull over it and revert by tomorrow? Will that work?"

Manoj, "Sure."

As you can see, there is a subtle difference. You can share your observations without calling it a pattern or calling out as you see it and explicitly stating that it is not a pattern.

These are some of the things I observed – however, I am still not sure which of these is a pattern.

Or

These are some of the things I observed; however, none of them is a pattern enough for me to call out at this point and make it feedback worthy.

> **So, you might start your feedback in the following manner:**
>
> "Here is my observation/Here is what I noticed"
>
> "Here is what I see"
>
> Share behavioural data, specifics here
>
> **And then focus on the issue, not the person**
>
> "The presentation was well structured, but could have been articulated better" (instead of your presentation was poor)

"Was an idea that was not elaborated upon" (and not "you did not elaborate on the idea")

"The quality of the data"

State "what that did to you" (impact)

"I was not able to understand the solution"

"I was wondering what happens next"

"The client stated that they were not clear on the features"

Once you have shared this, you can opt to Ask or Tell

And if you have improvements/suggestions – Tell

"I think better articulation will help"

"The idea needs to be elaborated upon in a manner that people understand what is expected of them"

"We need better data."

"We need data that is more comprehensive or sliced more granularly or grouped differently"

You can also "Ask" at this juncture. Ask narrow, open-ended questions as opposed to purely open-ended questions

"How to ensure that the reporting solutions are better understood?" (instead of what can we do better)

> "How can we drive home the point on service metrics better?"
>
> **Once this is done, you can talk on the timelines and next steps.**

TLDR: The purpose of feedback models is to give a structure to your conversation. Use simple models as a step to build your overall conversation skill. Make a habit of sharing feedback, observations, so that it can be strung into a pattern for the recipient – both appreciative and critical. Done well, in all likelihood, they are blind spots for your recipient. Try using SBI/SBI plus to give pattern-based feedback.

Chapter 7

Step in: Create a Culture of Feedback in Your Team

The Cast:

Vani: The boss

Manoj: Manager

Shalini: Manoj's peer manager who is new

Ashwin, Dheeraj: Manoj's team

Chetan, Sushma: Shalini's team

Tom is Vani's boss in the US. Tom manages both teams from the global office. One team, the India team, reports to Vani and the other team in the US, directly reports to him.

Manoj meets Vani.

Manoj: I need your guidance on this one.

Vani: Sure, how can I help?

Manoj: Dheeraj has recently had a conversation with Tom and it looks like Dheeraj is upset.

Vani: Did he tell you that?

Manoj: No, Ashwin did.

Vani: Hmm. And what is your dilemma?

Manoj: Well, I want to bring it up with Dheeraj, but if I bring it up, it becomes something that Ashwin shared with me. I don't know if Dheeraj wants to talk about it.

Vani: Have you asked him?

Manoj: No. Maybe I should ask him.

In general, when there is a need as a manager to step into a conversation, a slightly sticky conversation, our first instinct is to stay out. My experience with leaders suggests that the exact opposite works in building a culture of feedback in the team.

The best leaders Step in. If you have to create a culture of feedback in your team the only way is to role model the behaviour. This might sound prescriptive, but the next time you feel like stepping away from a conversation, fight that instinct and step in.

Stepping in:

Builds your skill – and each conversation makes the next conversation easier. Second, it builds your managerial courage of having the conversation.

And bonus: when you go in prepared and have a conversation, it makes a huge difference to the conversation outcome. Over time, your fears are conquered and your teams get used to such conversations

The perception of you changes over time to "She will have a conversation, each time she has something to share."

Or

"She will never avoid a conversation, and she is authentic (she says what she sees) and is vulnerable (if she is unsure, she states that she is unsure)."

It will be difficult initially. The first few times can be difficult and stressful. But each time you do it, you get better at it. And you can thank the so-called irrationals for having helped you out in your skill development.

Once you begin to use it, you will enjoy using the skill.

As you build this into a habit, you will notice that your team begins to respect you for your fairness, authenticity and professionalism.

Manoj: Dheeraj, Ashwin mentioned that you had a conversation with Tom and you were quite upset about it.

Dheeraj: Oh, is it?

Manoj: Would you like to talk about it?

Dheeraj: Well, I am not sure.

Manoj: What is the hesitation?

Dheeraj: I think I can sort out the issue myself. It is not worth your time I think.

Manoj: If time is the only concern, don't worry. I am happy to spend time discussing this with you.

Dheeraj: Yes, sure.

(Note: it is likely when Dheeraj says I don't want to waste your time – the unstated reason could also be that he feels Manoj might perceive him to be incompetent. And hence he uses time as an easy reason. It is worth probing that angle as well, but at this juncture, it is easier to allay his fear and open the door to a conversation.)

Here is what stepping in looks like:

Manoj: I spoke to Dheeraj and asked him if he was ok with me talking to Tom about how the team feels.

Vani: Anything you want from me?

Manoj: Just letting you know that I will be talking to Tom since this is about the team that is directly under him.

Vani: Sure, go ahead.

Encouraging team members to Step in

Dheeraj: Tom never supports us. If you notice, he agrees with us on the call, but when we have a common meeting, he always supports the development team.

Manoj: Why don't you bring it up with him?

D: No, I am not comfortable doing that. You are the manager, you bring it up.

M: I can bring this up with Tom. However, you have been in the thick of things, I would rather that you have the conversation. I will be present in the conversation as support. Will that work?

D: Not very sure.

M: This is the way I look at it. It is important to have conversations. Maybe he doesn't realize that this is happening. So let us share feedback with him. What do you think?

D: See, as long as it does not reflect badly on us as a team, I am ok with it.

M: I can assure you that it won't. This is an important conversation to have.

Dheeraj sets up the meeting with Tom and Manoj.

Manoj notices that while the conversation was set up for 30 minutes, for the first 15 minutes Dheeraj rambled on and on about how the project was going.

Manoj steps in, "Dheeraj, can we talk about the issue you wanted to discuss?"

D, "Yes, I was about to bring it up."

Tom, "What's the issue?"

D, "Nothing, Tom. Everything is good."

Manoj steps in:

"Tom, on two occasions in the last 10 days, when we had the testing review call, we had shared our approach and you had agreed, but in the joint meeting you went back on what we had agreed. This makes us look bad in front of the development team. Dheeraj, can you share the details."

Dheeraj went on to share details of occasion 1 and occasion 2.

Tom, "Appreciate your candid feedback. I did not realize this was happening. In my mind I was doing the right thing. Next time onwards, we will all have a joint meeting and come to agreement before we meet the business team."

D, "Great, thanks, Tom"

Tom, "Anything else?"

D, "No."

Tom, "If there is nothing else, thanks, and have a great weekend."

D, "You too."

Stepping in for in the moment feedback:

The call disconnected and Manoj called Dheeraj and asked, "What happened?"

"I was unable to share the issue."

"Yes, I could see that. What happened? We had spoken about it in detail and practiced it, so why did you develop cold feet?"

"I don't know."

"Hmm… I understand. It happens. But often leaders have blind spots; it is our job to bring it to their notice and in all probability they will take it well. So it is worth an attempt."

> Feedback is best delivered as close to the point of occurrence as possible. And this simple action contributes/highly to team member engagement. Why? Because the team member feels cared for enough to be given constant feedback.
>
> One factor of team member engagement is how much feedback the team member receives on a regular basis. There is another term for it – in the moment feedback. Spot coaching is another widely used term to denote feedback in real time.
>
> If you can start "in the moment" feedback with your team members – and start with appreciative feedback – it allows you to build trust and get better with your technique. And you have a highly engaged team.
>
> Moments of truth: We often talk about moments of truth when it comes to consumer experiences. On similar lines, think of interaction moments that you have with your team. If every interaction makes them feel appreciated, cared for, supported, they will look forward to every interaction with you. And what's more, the answer to first question that we started this book with – your manager

> has called you, what goes on in your mind – will change from apprehension to curiosity. And you build a transparent relationship with your team – where everyone is clear about their roles, get clear, honest, regular feedback and work towards team goals. This sounds like utopia, but it is not. And the single step towards that is regular, recurring, meaningful, feedback.

How can you step in as a Leader? How can you get your team to be truly transparent with each other? A few years ago we were a team working on a consulting assignment and I found it difficult working with one of the team members. And as consultants, with significant experience in this space – having conversations is relatively easy. So, I shared my concerns with the leader of the group.

She listened to me patiently and promised to close loop on this. And she did. She took my points, discussed with the other consultant and came back with a resolution. But before she did so, she asked me if I would like this feedback to be shared with the other consultant. (I said yes.) She also asked me if I was comfortable sharing this with the consultant myself. (I said no.) The reason was the person was unknown to me at the time; whereas the leader knew the consultant much better. And as it turned out, she had heard similar things from her team members in the past. So she was able to bring this up with the consultant more easily than I could have. The specific issue got resolved during that assignment simply because the leader was able to offer the safe space to express feedback and bring all of us on the same page. More importantly she did that "in the moment."

This was a moment of truth for me in working with this leader. And I hold her in high esteem and we have worked on many assignments together since then.

When you lead a high powered team: You are a leader – How can you Step in?

Let us look at the examples of two distinct teams.

Team 1: A Product team at the forefront of developing 0 to 1 products for the company, focused on research and innovation. Brainstorming sessions and iteration meetings called for careful examination of diverse views and thoughts of people involved and converging on next steps to keep up the momentum and meet the committed product-launch prototype, testing and launch timelines agreed with the business teams.

Team 2: A senior regional leadership team (comprising the Vice Presidents) dealing with the ongoing challenge of supporting country-level initiatives led by the Country Head and remaining aligned to the demands of their global leadership team.

For both the teams, the task was to create a culture of candid feedback. Because the teams had experts (functional/business) it was important for the team to be candid in sharing feedback. If they did not, the teams risked losing money, time and competitive advantage. If they agreed or disagreed on something, they had to be able to give clear feedback, resolve disagreements and have productive conflict.

How to get peers warmed up to the idea of having candid conversations? How to appreciate each other without feeling insecure? How to give feedback to each other without making it personal? How to discuss matters keeping the organization in perspective and avoid personal egos? Overall, each of these questions pointed towards creating certain ways of working such as not holding back from each other, agreeing to disagree and giving 100% for the initiative.

This meant building the skill to give feedback to each other that is issue focused, candid and has the best interests of the organization in mind. The leader had to be at the forefront of this process, taking active interest and being a part of every discussion. By stepping in, he sets the tone for the program and signals his commitment to step in in future as well.

So, they worked on building this "way of working." It had to be on the foundation of "trust." They went through a series of workshops that enabled them to build their skills through live exercises. It took a while, and the teams modelled themselves into a unit that would share candid feedback.

> What about trust?
>
> Shouldn't you win the team's trust before you Step in and give feedback? How will they accept feedback if they can't trust you?
>
> Start with the action of giving and seeking regular feedback and trust will build through the process.

One of the key things to remember in Stepping in is intent. What is your intent in sharing feedback?

Opportunities for feedback are to be treated as learning moments – and not to establish one's superiority. Feedback should not be about making a point. "I told you so" – verbally or nonverbally is not feedback.

The need to give feedback should not have anything to do with the fact that you are higher on the hierarchy or an expert. The need to share feedback is about offering a genuine developmental opportunity.

As you practice Stepping in, you build on your coaching skills.

The ability to give good actionable feedback, asking questions and receiving feedback on a constant basis is a fantastic building block towards honing one's coaching skills.

Tip: *The Coaching Habit*, by Michael Bungay Stanier, breaks coaching into a simple list of 7 questions. It is one of best and easiest books to read to see how feedback conversations can be a lead into good basic coaching conversations. And with just 7 questions you can change your conversations.[9]

TLDR: Do not resist conversations. Have conversations. As a leader most of what you do is have conversations. So, the sooner you learn to step in to conversations, the better. Use feedback conversations to build your skill of having conversations. Step in into a conversation you would normally avoid – and repeat.

Chapter 8

The Ultimate Conversation Framework

The Cast:

Vani: The boss

Manoj: Manager

Shalini: Manoj's peer manager who is new

Ashwin, Dheeraj: Manoj's team

Chetan, Sushma: Shalini's team

Vani, "Do you know what is a smart way to have conversations?"

Shalini, "Ask questions?"

V, "Yes, and …"

S, "Once you ask questions, see if they have a good idea about the topic at hand, fill in anything they missed."

V, "Yes, and …"

S, "Once the problem is established, quickly move into solution and see if they have an idea of the solution. If they do, go with it, else, add in your bit."

V, "Perfect."

S, "And then agree, close and talk about next steps. But I have a question – why are questions good?"

V, "What happens when you ask a question?"

S, "I pause. And think."

V, "And what is happening there?"

S, "I have to use my mind."

V, "Yes, exactly, good questions help people access their own thinking."

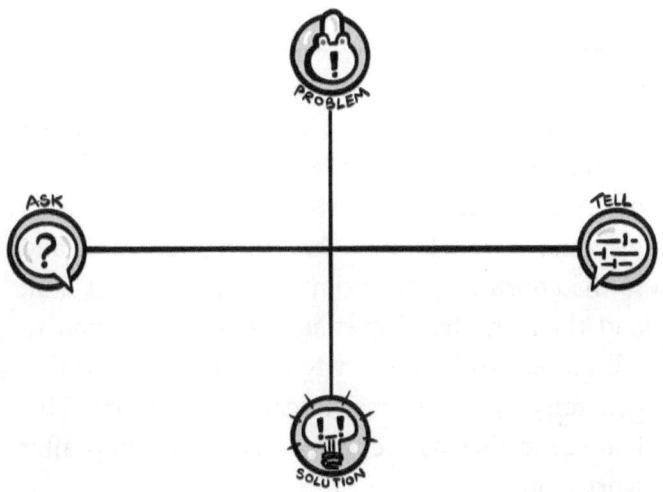

The above image is adapted from David Rock's *Quiet Leadership*,[10] where he lays out this conversation framework in the context of coaching. However, the framework is a very effective method that can be used in every daily feedback conversation. Building this habit of keeping the framework in your mind builds your overall conversation skills and your team gets used to thinking in this mode. This is not just my experience but also the experience of others that I have trained using this approach.

The ultimate conversation framework works like this ...

There is an Ask and Tell axis and there is a Problem and Solution axis.

One of the first barriers to cross is to move from Tell to Ask.

> Generally, managers and leaders tend to "Tell" more. In my workshops, I ask this question. What do we, as managers and leaders, tend to do more of: Ask or Tell? Almost immediately comes a response – we ask more. And then a few more add to the chorus. At this point, I wait, pause for a bit and then one hand goes up, "I think we tend to tell more." And then slowly realization dawns that generally as managers we tend to tell more. This is a scene that has repeated itself workshop after workshop.

Why do we tend to tell more?

Because Tell is easy. Tell saves time. Also your reportees and team members expect you to tell. By authority or hierarchy, you are expected to "Tell." Therefore, Tell is easy. It is also satisfying – you go to bed thinking, "Yes, I resolved many issues today."

Why is Ask difficult?

For one, it is counter-intuitive. You have to ask, wait for others to respond, guide their thoughts, change their perception, so it is some amount of work. They may not get the answer right away, they may go around in circles, or they may not have the knowledge or the experience. Besides, as a manager, if you "ask" too much, your team may perceive you as someone who lacks knowledge.

Today, teams have the capacity to think. And teams are often smarter than managers when it comes to certain skills. So, why not get them to think and in the process, build one's team capability?

Secondly, if you, as manager, have to solve all problems, you are the bottleneck. Your team has to wait for you to think, decide, arrive at resolutions. The team will only be as fast as you. And that is suboptimal.

How is "Ask" the solution?

Ask enables your teams to think. By "asking," the team feels their opinion is valued – and therefore they begin to think. Over time as you practice this the team begins to get used to "Ask" and contribute to the thinking process. And yes, in the short run, it will take more time to take decisions if you use the "Ask" route.

Does that mean I only "Ask" never "Tell"?

It does not have to be that way. There are situations where as a manager you have to take decisions, take a stand. In case of a crisis, when something has to be accomplished soon, as a manager you are required to take charge, give direction, check commitment and take certain calls. Such situations definitely require the use of "Tell." At all other times, you can use "Ask."

Now that we have seen the advantage of "Ask" over "Tell," let's take a look at the Problem–Solution axis.

A lot of times managers tend to focus on problems rather than solutions. This is more so in legacy cultures and industries. It may not be so true in newer companies and cultures, but the overall focus on the problem side of things is human nature. Try to shift your focus to solutions rather than problems.

Caveat: You can still go wrong if you continue to use "Ask" in the problem quadrant and "Tell" in the solution quadrant.

So, let's combine the two axes and examine each quadrant.

Ask, Problem: Time spent asking about the problem – Interrogation.

Ask, Solution: Time spent asking about the solution – Invitation.

Tell, Problem: Time spent telling about the problem – Information

Tell, Solution: Time spent telling about the solution – Instruction

Let us see how a feedback conversation can flow across these quadrants.

Start from the Ask/Problem quadrant.

A lot of times, your team knows what the problem is.

Move to Tell/Problem to state your view and to add anything that was missed.

S: "Chetan, how do you think the meeting with the client went?"

C: "I think it was ok, but there were one or two things I would want to do better since she did not seem fully convinced."

S: "Hmm ... go on."

C: "So, while the overall meeting was good and the client did seem to like our experience profile and the solution, there are some gaps in our solution portfolio itself. The client wanted more data points before being convinced that we had answers to all her questions."

S: "Hmmm. You are right. In addition to that, I felt we had not understood her need clearly." [Ensure that you state your view.]

C: "Ok."

From there move to the Ask/Solution quadrant. There is a good chance your team has an idea of the solution. Or you get an insight in the direction your team is thinking.

Move to Tell/Solution quadrant if required. [Break glass in case of fire.]

Continuing from above ...

S: *"So, what do you think can be the way forward?"*

C: *"The first thing is to clarify the needs with every client. Perhaps relook at the questionnaire we share with clients at the start of an engagement. Also, add a couple of data to support the point being made. I think we have those, but we have not thought of it to be important enough to be shared with clients."*

S: *"Could you give me an example?"*

C: *"Yes, the new features already cover more than what she asked, but since we had stated them all, it appeared as if our solution was not meeting her needs."*

S: *"Yes, I think we should present this to the client once we make the changes, so that she sees that we indeed have a solution for her. We can also seek her initial feedback that may be very useful for us."*

Always remember to close!

S: *"Does that make sense? What do you think?"*

C: *"Yes, it does."*

S: *"So what are the next steps?"*

C: *"I will come back to you with the completed proposal."*

S: *"How much time do you reckon that will take?"*

C: *"In a day's time. And then we set up time with the client to walk her through the revised proposal. I need a little more time to work on the new questionnaire. Give me a week to close on that."*

S: "Great, thanks!"

Possibly one thought running in your mind is, how can it be so easy? Try it out. You will realize that 80–90% of your conversations will be as easy as above.

What might go wrong and how can you work around?

Scenario 1:

S: "Can you tell me how the meeting with the client went?"

C: "It was fantastic (this is an irrational persona)*"*

Continue Ask mode:

S: "I am curious, what about it was fantastic?"

Option 1: *C: "Everything."* [Clearly delusional – Switch to tell. Share your point of view with specific data.]

Option 2: *C: "I played my part well, there are a few other things we need to improve as a team."* [Congratulations, you have hired a narcissist]

Option 2: *S: "Why do you think you did well? What do you think the team needs to improve on?"*

S: "Hmmm, I had a different observation. There were gaps in the solution portfolio and some data points were missing. The client validated that. Do you still feel we did not miss anything?"

[If the observations are pertinent, add to it with "Tell." Else, switch to Tell.]

Usually, at this juncture because you have pressed on the point, the person will see reason. If the person still disagrees, likely you have found someone in the irrational 1%.

S: "So, what is the way forward according to you?"

Option 1: C: "I don't know, you tell me." [The irrational 1%]

Option 2: C: "I think the team needs to play its part."

S: "I am sure you have a point of view – with your level of experience." [Appeal to intelligence.]

or

S: "I am intrigued with the 'I don't know.' Why don't you think of something and come back?" [Push the case with a time.]

or

S: "I have asked a couple of other members to come back with a plan. If you don't have a view, we will go with what they come back with." [Appeal to intelligence and ego.]

or

S: "Let me be specific. Is there something you can do?" [Get specific as to whose responsibility it is.]

Over time you can start directly in the Ask-Solution quadrant.

> Sometimes in a feedback conversation, the recipient might not agree right away. Regardless of the immediate agreement, the discussion will set off a line of thinking. Be prepared to have a follow-up conversation to explore the thinking. The effects of switching from Tell to Ask are cumulative.

If you move to the tell quadrant, use the SBI (or equivalent) model. Use SBI on the Problem and the Solution side. You can also use the SBI+ model in both cases.

On the Ask/Problem quadrant stick to what questions rather than who questions. [Except, what do you think – which is almost always a good question.] Keep the focus of the "Ask" on the issue not the person.

> In the Ask-Solution mode – I find David Rocks 3 level framework very useful.
>
> ... when is a self-directed approach going to be useful:- any time you feel you are about to give advice, or about to tell a person what you would do, or wanting to share your experience or opinion. If it seems appropriate to do this, it's generally going to be appropriate to use a self-directed approach.
>
> There are instances when a pure self-directed approach is not going to work. There is a ladder

of approaches here, from 100% self-directed, to partially self-directed. Always start at the pure self-directed "Ask" first before resorting to "tell" in any form …

The summary of the three approaches is as follows

Approach 1: Help Someone Make New Connections on the Spot (by asking questions on the spot)

Approach 2: Help Someone Make New Connections Later (by fixing a time later)

Approach 3: If Neither of These Approaches Is Possible, Provide an Answer in a Way That's Most Useful to the Person's Thinking [David Rock, *Quiet Leadership*]

As you can see, "Tell" is the last option. Over time, your team begins to get used to this line of conversation and begins to "think," thereby getting to become more independent.

Here are a few more pointers on the nature of the conversation because, even with a good framework, certain missteps can ruin the conversation.

The conversation has to be authentic. An authentic conversation is one where both parties can say what they feel or share their point of view. It is not repeating the same point again and again. It is not conversations without specific inputs (and often data). It has to connect and create meaning for the person who receives it.

Beware of the Tell that masquerades as Ask.

"Did you not work on the idea I told you to?" or "Why are you not moving forward on the discussion?"

In the first, the idea has already been told (ideally, it should be the team's idea), and you just want the team to work on it.

In the second, you have decided that they are not moving forward on the discussion.

Both are not genuine Asks.

Here are a few options:

"Any update on our idea since we spoke about it?" or "Where are you on this idea after we last spoke about it? Do you need any support from me?"

"What's the update on our last discussion?" or "What are your discoveries about the idea we last spoke about? Where are you on it now?"

Regardless of "Ask" or "Tell" to say there has to be trust, empathy and a tone that conveys that.

For instance: [Tell]

Vani: I appreciate you trying to fit into the culture of the organization given that you are just six months old here and I can see that you are facing some issues as you go through the process. Wanted to share with you that it is normal to face teething issues and I don't want you to unnecessarily worry about it.

For instance: [Ask]

Vani: How is it going with you?

Shalini: Well, been having a tough time to be honest and I am expecting some feedback from you on the same.

Vani: I understand. More than feedback, I want to know what you feel.

Shalini: I am not sure. I am new here, but I wish it was faster. I get the feeling that things are not moving and it is frustrating.

Vani: See, I am sure as you spend more time and both the people here and you get used to each other, assimilation will happen. Is there something I can do to help?

Shalini: No, nothing at this point, but perhaps in a week's time, I might come to you for specific help.

What is the difference between constructive feedback and criticism and how does that map to Ask and Tell?

Typically, criticism falls in the Tell category and Constructive Feedback can be a mix of Ask and Tell.

Constructive feedback, while pointing out an issue, has evidence, specificity and offers support on the way forward. Constructive feedback, while calling out the issue, is rooted in support and generosity and looks at way forward. This can be done in both Ask and Tell mode.

Criticism on the other hand sounds like "That's a stupid movie." Criticism costs nothing, has zero commitment except the intent to pull someone down without any resource. Criticism is an opinion. A Judgement. There is no support. No generosity. And it does not recommend a way forward.

If that sounds harsh, yes, the intent to share it in that manner is to reassure you that we are interested in constructive feedback, not criticism.

Criticism:

Vani: "Shalini, the last delivery was a disaster. In the customer acceptance testing, 22 defects showed up. This is extremely irresponsible behaviour. I am disappointed with the team and those responsible can expect a lower rating."

Constructive feedback (Tell):

V: "How do you think the last delivery was?"

S: "Not good at all. "

V: "Yes, in the customer acceptance testing, 22 defects showed up. That is 15 more than what it should have been."

S: "Yes."

V: "Did you see the report?"

S: "Yes."

V: "Can you see the report and come back to me with a first cut approach on how we will ensure this will not be repeated?"

S: "Sure."

V: "I hope you realize that deliveries like these will push down our Customer Scores and encourage the competition to step in. Once you are ready with the plan, we will jointly review it and deploy it immediately. What do you think?"

S: "Agreed."

[Note the receiver has very little to say except to agree – though this feedback is delivered in Tell style, it is not criticism and is not a bad way to deliver feedback because it follows the CORBS framework.]

Constructive feedback (Ask):

V: "Wanted to talk to you about the last delivery. How do you reckon it went?"

S: "In my opinion, the last delivery was a disaster, Vani. In the customer acceptance testing, 22 defects showed up. That is 15 more than what it should have been. I saw the report and it's not encouraging."

V: "So what do you think we can do about it?"

S: "Obviously, something would have broken at our end. My first hunch is, it is the requirements – we might have missed something. I will come back with an analysis and a first cut approach on gaps."

V: "I do hope you see the concern with a large defect number."

S: "Yes, J is an important new customer and this does not help from a long-term confidence perspective. Let me come back with the gaps."

V: "How would you like me to help?"

S: "Let us review it jointly to ensure that nothing is missed."

V: "Sure. By when can you come back with the plan?"

S: "I think I can come back to you by EOD tomorrow."

[Notice the solution is from the recipient – and hence leads to greater ownership and accountability. Also notice the gentle nature of the feedback.]

Criticism:

Vani: There is no improvement on your Customer Engagement score.

Constructive Feedback:

Vani: *Shalini, I was going over your Customer Engagement score and I noticed that the score is the same as last time. I wonder what is going on and if you would like to talk about it?*

Shalini: Sure.

Vani: *I want to assure you that I believe in you – you have been a high performer for a few years now – and I will do all I can to support you, but I need to know from you if there is anything I can do to help.*

[This is an example, but when it happens, constructive feedback will be a conversation while criticism will be a monologue followed by silence or acceptance, but no conviction.]

Reaction: Shalini opens up.

Shalini: Yes, I am actually quite upset with this. We had put in so much effort as a team. I think there are a couple of issues. This technology is new to us and I am not fully comfortable with this, nor is the team. The last update did throw in a few bugs that resulted in service outages that were twice more than usual. I think that is the main issue.

Vani: Hmm. How do you think we can mitigate this?

Shalini: First is not to accept new releases without a staging test. The second is to train the new members fully so that we don't spend time learning during the release week (for the record, this was a big issue last week).

Vani: Hmmm, sounds like you have thought about it. Anything else?

Shalini: Also thinking if it is worth having a conversation with the customer on this issue and share the plan with them as well?

Vani: I think that is a good idea. So Shalini, based on this conversation, when do you think you can come back with a plan? And how often can it be reviewed to ensure that we are on top of it?

Shalini: Give me a couple of days.

Empathetic conversations work because it is two-way dialogue that enables the giver and the receiver of feedback to be on the same plane.

Does feedback have to be different for Creative people?

When I say creative, I mean creative people or experts in their own field – like Technologists,

Designers, Graphic artists and so on. They are likely to be individual contributors or subject matter experts.

This is the future of work where increasingly people you work with will be experts and will know more than you. How to tap into their expertise and enable them to contribute better using better feedback techniques?

Understand the difference between Critique and Feedback

Start with Ask – with the focus on the goal. That ensures that you know you are working towards the same objective. And evaluate how the goal is being met.

Signal that your feedback is an opinion and then share your feedback.

Next Ask for a solution. Respect their expertise. If you "tell" the solution, it might not work well because you are not an "expert."

Give away the impulse to control (they are in charge of the work – you are in charge of the plan).

Feedback to provide trajectories rather than definitive paths.

Describe what is working, in detail (Here is what is working for me …).

Ask questions out of genuine curiosity: What do you think? Where could we go next with this? How could we touch this aspect? (signalling you are open to ideas other than your own).

Make sure that your questions are borne out of interest. And the CORBS framework remains.

The key is to remember that creative folks are specifically valued for their expertise. And it requires a higher degree of empathy to ensure that the expertise is acknowledged and tapped into.

To summarize:

Identify the specific aspect of the idea being analyzed.

Relate that to an objective or best practice (the goal is agreed upon).

Describe how and why the aspect or decision works to support or not support the objective or best practice.

Follow that up with what it does to you, "I am not able to understand" (as opposed to this does not work).

Generally, stick to the issue – the "what" rather than the "who" (this rule is constant everywhere).

Watch out for these pitfalls:

All questions are not equal. Some questions are answers disguised as questions. E.g.: "Why don't you try using the new version?"

Watch out for close-ended questions – they are not questions, they are opinions disguised with a question mark. E.g.: "Did you check the defect log from yesterday?"

Beware of the fake "we." E.g.: Why don't we go over it and share our findings tomorrow. Unless you intend to actually do this together this is a fake "we." The better framing would be a candid, "Go over it and share a set of findings tomorrow."

The tone can give away the lack of empathy though the words sound empathetic.

Watch out for the Yes, but. "Yes, that a great idea but I see a few issues." This is not agreement – this is a deflection that the idea not that good. So, get rid of the yes, but and ask a curious question or two.

Are you really listening?

TLDR: Ask, while it takes effort, is a far effective way of starting conversations than Tell. Over time, it becomes a habit for both you and your team.

The art of asking the right questions is far better than the art of having the right answers. A well-framed question will get you far ahead than the best answer. And, specifically, asking the clarifying question is a secret weapon in any conversation. Consciously practice using the Conversation Framework in your feedback conversations.

Chapter 9

The Counter-Intuitive Way

The Cast:

Vani: The boss

Manoj: Manager

Shalini: Manoj's peer who is new

Ashwin, Dheeraj: Manoj's team

Chetan, Sushma: Shalini's team

There is a well-known scene in the movie *Cars 1*: a conversation between two cars. It happens as the protagonist, Lightning McQueen, is learning to race on dirt tracks.

Doc Hudson: I'll put it simple: if you're going hard enough left, you'll find yourself turning right.

Lightning McQueen: Oh, right. That makes perfect sense. Turn right to go left.

And in the context of Feedback, this is the left turn to go right: The more you appreciate your team the easier it is for you to share critical feedback.

Shalini, "I can't imagine appreciating Chetan."

Manoj, "Why not?"

S, "If I did, he would go ballistic and demand a promotion from me."

M, "Is it?"

S, "Yes."

M, "Why would that be?"

S, "It's my assumption based on previous experiences with Chetan."

M, "Hmm. What about it?"

S, "Well, he is always so combative/self-righteous I just can't imagine it."

M, "And what are your thoughts on him now?"

S, "Simply put, I prefer to avoid him rather than engage with him. I engage only when absolutely necessary."

The moment there is that first sign of friction with someone, your conversations drop, appreciation drops still further and you tend to disconnect from or ignore that team member. This is natural human behaviour – and not that it is justified, but this is how it happens.

It is possible that there might be people on your team that you would rather lose, in which case you might choose to indulge in this behaviour. And seen through that lens, it may even be a way of rationalizing that behaviour. But, perhaps there is a better way that has escaped our attention.

> Another common Indian trait, we find it difficult to take it when we are appreciated. We also find it difficult to appreciate, for that matter. The younger generation may be better off, but current research gives us a rather poor score for appreciation.
>
> Tip: Try appreciating your parents or maid or driver – they will actually find it difficult to take it.

Vani, "So, does your team feel appreciated?"

Manoj, "Of course."

Shalini, "Pretty sure they do."

Vani, "Do you feel appreciated?"

Both, "Yes, of course."

Vani, "So, how do you appreciate your teams, if you could share with me?"

M, "By taking the team out for lunch."

S, "By writing congratulatory emails marked to the team/US office/Other peers."

M, "Rewards."

S, "That's all I can think of."

M, "What else is required? The team does its job everyday – and gets paid. Isn't that enough?"

It is difficult to give appreciative feedback – in general and specifically as Indians. [Confession: It has been difficult for me as well and it has been an acquired skill.]

> In my workshops, there is a pattern as to how this conversation flows.
>
> "I want you to reflect upon the question – Do you appreciate your teams enough?"
>
> There is a moment of thought and then almost immediately, instantly, participants react, of course yes. We appreciate our teams.
>
> "And are you appreciated enough by your leaders?" Again, the answers fly in thick and past.
>
> And then I go silent. I wait. I ask them to think about it, do you think your teams feel appreciated enough? Do you feel appreciated enough?
>
> They respond with silence and then usually a lone voice pipes up, "No, I don't think so" and then another one says, "I am not sure if we did it will have the right effect" and then, all by themselves the room settles into a stable equilibrium where almost all participants state, "I think we can get better at appreciating our teams."

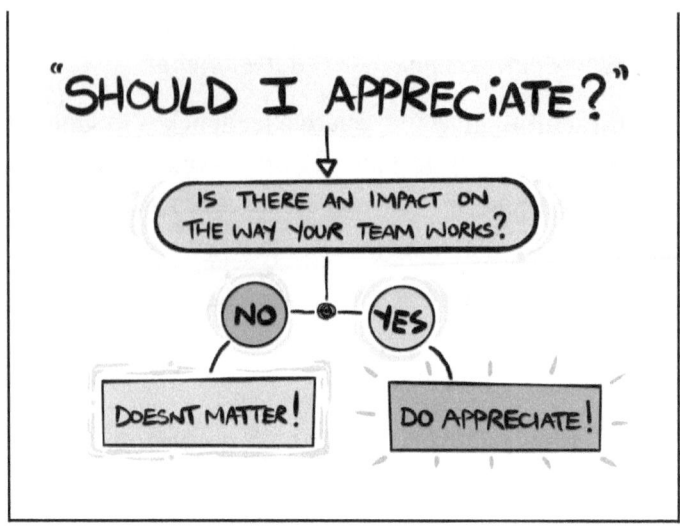

We don't appreciate our teams enough. And I don't mean, general pink-eyed optimism, appreciating for "the fabulous font on the presentation," and the rewards and recognition, but authentic positive strokes. Most teams don't feel appreciated enough for the work they do – and that includes most of us. Think of the last person on your team. Think of those on the field. Think of those in the middle of your bell curve. Do they feel appreciated?

Indeed – most of our family members also don't feel appreciated on a day-to-day basis. Our lives are devoid of positive strokes. David Rock says, "People get on average, a couple of minutes of positive feedback each year versus thousands of hours of negative feedback."[11]

It is important to both acknowledge and act on it. At the risk of overdoing it, positive strokes are still worth it, given our traits.

> What is a stroke?
>
> Eric Berne describes Stroke as a fundamental unit of social transaction. An exchange of strokes constitutes a transaction, which is the unit of social intercourse. (Berne, 1964)[12] A stroke is a unit of recognition, when one person recognizes another person. A stroke can be physical, verbal or non-verbal and hence could be a hand shake, a compliment or a nod. It could also be a "Hello," "Go away!" or a dismissive wave of the hand. All of these acknowledge that the other person exists.
>
> There is a great variety of stroke needs and styles in the world – this is the result of differences in wealth, culture and parenting methods – but all these can be divided into two big categories of strokes: positive strokes and negative strokes. These can be conditional, or unconditional.
>
> Berne also reasoned that any stroke, be it positive or negative, is better than no strokes at all.
>
> For example, if you are walking in front of your house and you see your neighbour, you will likely smile and say "Hi." Your neighbour will likely say "hello" back. This is an example of a positive stroke. Your neighbour could also frown at you and say nothing. This is an example of a negative

stroke. But either case is better than no stroke at all, if your neighbour ignored you completely.

As far as "conditional" and "unconditional" strokes are concerned, Berne stated that unconditional strokes are related to what you are (strokes for being), while conditional strokes are about what you do (strokes for doing).

Below are some examples of the different types of strokes:

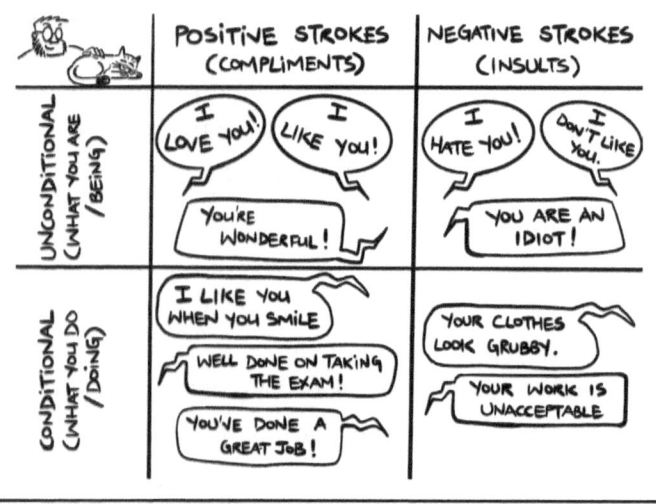

7 levels of Positive Feedback

1. Appreciation[13]:

    What it sounds like: "I really appreciate you completing that report on time."

    This is the first level of positive feedback. Unfortunately, the best thing people hear is

"Good job" or "Great job." And nothing beyond that. Think of this as an acknowledgement of something well done. While this is important, as a leader one has to go beyond this level of feedback. Secondly, it is important for leaders to be able to distinguish the levels of positive feedback in their own minds.

2. Validation:

   What it sounds like: "I can see you've given this report a lot of thought and attention."

   Validation is a form of communicating acceptance and building trust in a team member. Many times team members require validation – that they are important, that their work is noticed and important. This is a way to provide that support.

3. Recognition:

   What it sounds like: "It's clear you are a very talented problem-solver."

   When we think recognition, we often think of Reward and Recognition and of something that has to be given. But to hear about how one's work has helped the team/organization/peers in a beneficial manner can be uplifting For instance, knowing that I was recognized as a "creative" person among my peers was a huge booster for me.

4. Affirmation:

   What it sounds like: "I think you deserve all the credit for this month's project."

Affirmation is the stamp on something done well. This is something that leaders rarely do, which is why it is valuable in your toolkit. As Indians, we find it difficult to accept positive strokes, so this one is worth practicing.

5. Confirmation:

What it sounds like: "It's great you took on this project, it suited your style."

This is really #3 and #4 combined into a deeper positive stroke. It is an assertion of good decision and good execution.

6. Thanking:

What it sounds like: "Thanks for taking the time to focus 100% on this project."

It might sound trivial, but saying thanks has a huge multiplier effect. Do it on mail, on WhatsApp or in person and it has a greater feeling, but do it nonetheless. We think as leaders, we have thanked them, but this is just a good thing to do and it adds coins in your positive strokes good-will box.

Some excuses I have heard (from managers) in my workshops on why they do not appreciate their team members:

Team might become complacent/take it easy.

Team performance will go down.

Team might come back with all the appreciation and seek a higher rating/promotion/salary hike.

Team will take me for granted.

I appreciate them when it is required.

We are all doing a job, no appreciation is required.

I am not appreciated, why should I appreciate?

Employees get paid – what will appreciation do additionally.

We are not in kindergarten where we appreciate people for trivial things.

Why appreciate them for doing their job or doing their job well? That's their job.

We appreciate people when they do something terrific (like winning a Nobel, maybe?).

Tip: Use Positive feedback as Learning moments.

In the book, *Radical Candor*,[14] Kim Scott divides a manager's relationship into 4 quadrants: Manipulative insincerity, Ruinous empathy, Radical

Candor and Obnoxious Aggression. The axes are divided into Care Personally and Challenge directly.

In Manipulative Insincerity – you don't Challenge, nor do you Care.

In Ruinous Empathy – you don't Challenge, and Care a lot (ostensibly).

In the Obnoxious Aggression quadrant – you Challenge directly, but don't Care.

In the Radical Candor box – you care enough about your team and challenge them sufficiently enough.

If you notice, it is all about appreciating your team at the right times and giving them the tough feedback when it matters. And as part of the methodology stated in the book, you actually cannot move to Radical Candor unless you learn to appreciate with candor (ask yourself, how many of us do that) and learn to take criticism with candor (ditto).

In her book *Radical Candor*, Kim Scott describes a model of the same name for how to approach giving feedback in one-on-ones, weekly or otherwise, using the trusty 2 × 2 matrix

The two axes for this matrix are "challenge directly" and "care personally." When you give feedback to someone, you can give it in a vague, abstract way ("I think you could do a better job at communication"), or in a specific, actionable way where you challenge directly ("This sentence you said was confusing, here's why, and here's what I think you should have said"). Being vague and abstract is much easier to do because it avoids the hard work of identifying specific examples and the psychological stress of debating the nuances around those specifics. Many people thus take the easy way out. But for your feedback to be effective, you are going to need specifics. Caring personally involves nurturing the relationship you've built prior to giving feedback. If you've consistently shown that you have this person's best interests at heart, then you've laid the groundwork for that person to be receptive to your constructive criticism. On the other hand, if you don't have much of a relationship at all, or worse, have a negative one, your feedback is not likely to be accepted. It is too easy at that point for the receiver to disregard it. Radical candor is giving feedback in a way that it both challenges directly and cares personally (upper right quadrant of the matrix). Your feedback is completely candid and gets to the root of an issue, its radical form. It goes hand in hand with deliberate practice because this type of feedback is exactly the type that should be given in a deliberate practice session: a specific account of what the person could be doing better at a particular skill they are trying to improve. The other quadrants create suboptimal feedback patterns: Ruinous empathy (upper left quadrant) – when you care personally but don't challenge directly. This occurs when you aren't specific

> enough in your feedback. Obnoxious aggression (lower right quadrant) – when you challenge directly but don't care personally. This type of feedback is often brushed off because the lack of caring can make it seem insincere.
>
> Manipulative insincerity (lower left quadrant) – when you neither challenge directly nor care personally. This takes the form of vague criticism that isn't actionable enough to be useful and can be off-putting because of the lack of a strong foundational relationship.

APPRECIATE MORE TO BE ABLE TO SHARE ALL KINDS OF FEEDBACK!

Why is appreciation so important?

This is partly psychological – and partly real. Psychological because, when you as a manager speak to your team members on a regular basis about what is going well and what is not, they know you care. Real because having these conversations require effort and the effect is felt only when the conversations are authentic and genuine. It requires effort (and a certain degree of empathy) to have conversations again and again. It means you care enough to put that level of effort.

And as you use the conversation framework regularly, team members can see that the leader means well for them because they have a spectrum of conversations. They experience, "I am appreciated," "my opinions are valued" and "I am given regular feedback from a development lens." They can see that they have an "impartial" manager interested in building their skills beyond the immediate deliverable. They can see your authentic, vulnerable side.

And as you practice doing this, you can have any critical/developmental conversation easily simply because your reportees get all other types of feedback, not just critical.

Usually, if they had 5 conversations with their manager in the last 5 months, they are all developmental, 100% negative. The moment they have 50 more (or 30 or even 10) appreciative conversations, it is far easier to have 5 developmental conversations.

That is what makes it counter-intuitive. The more you engage with your team, talk to them, appreciate them, the easier it is for you to have difficult conversations.

S, "So yes, over the last few weeks, I had a couple of good conversations with Chetan."

M, "Good to know."

S, "Actually his work is quite good and there were a couple of places where he could have been genuinely appreciated. So, I told him that. He was surprised. And on his own accord and without my asking he ended up sharing something he could do differently/better."

Manoj smiled.

S, "I think it will get easier for me to have conversations with them. I will keep this momentum going."

Also over time the team trusts your intent. When your sole intent in giving feedback is to enable your team's growth, enable them to meet the team and organization goals and help them succeed, you will be able to share feedback of all kinds. This process builds trust. And, higher the trust, the easier it is for you to share feedback. [Note: Building trust is a long road, so don't expect any short term miracles.]

If you experience hesitation in sharing feedback with anyone on your team, keep this in mind.

Tip: Keep the appreciation authentic.

> Do not appreciate them for something that is not connected with their work at all. Appreciate their skills, their strengths that they demonstrate at work. Appreciating their singing skills at a party

and then dinging them for work does not earn brownie points as an authentic appreciation at work. An authentic conversation, for instance, will appreciate them for the hard work they put in, but also have clear call outs on the effectiveness of it, the good behaviour that should repeat and the behaviour that needs to change.

There is this herd behaviour that happens when the leader sends an appreciation mail marking all direct reports. And then they start off a reply-all thread congratulating the person for the achievement.

In this context someone shared a story with me – it is an apocryphal story. In an IT services firm, once a customer sent an appreciation mail – the onsite engineer duly forwarded it to the account manager, who in turn created an appreciation thread. Until finally someone bothered to read the bottom most email – the mail that had sparked off the thread – the mail said "thank you for clearing the paper jam in the printer."

I once had a manager who appreciated us for practically everything – and I was overjoyed when it started. As it turned out most of the appreciation was aimed at showing his boss how good a manager she was and how productive the team was. On any given day we could expect to receive a "good job" mail for almost anything copied to the boss. And almost none of the appreciation

> translated into performance conversations – because we never got actionable, real, usable feedback, nor were these appreciations used as a means to build a culture of amplifying best practices.
>
> The "real" feedback that was shared was almost always when something went wrong and she was shown in poor light in front of her manager. Whenever that happened, we would be subject to an outburst with an indignant tone of "I have always been telling you this." This sort of mindless appreciation is a facade for someone who does not have the skill to have a real feedback conversation.
>
> The appreciation was an attempt to appear to be a "nice guy" or a "nice manager" or a "pleasing personality." So, the appreciation did not help us get better – neither did we get actionable feedback. Over time the value of those appreciations went down and team members would simply disregard it because there was no meaning in those appreciations.

Practice building a culture of appreciation by role modelling it. Appreciate your team in a genuine manner. Have more brainstorming conversations. Talk to them about how they can get better at something. Have learning conversations when things go well. Enable them to get better at what they do. Talk to them about the strengths that you have observed them demonstrate. Make them more self-aware. In order to appreciate better, note that you will have to up the ante on your observation skills.

So, practice having genuinely appreciative conversations.

And what would you have to do for that? Observe more. Know their work better. Ask more. Mentor them more. And enable them to build their skills.

When you want to share critical or developmental feedback that lands well, ensure that you have shared appreciative feedback all the way along and that you are not there just to deliver bad news …

******

What if there was a lot of effort but the end result was not achieved? As a manager you still need to appreciate the effort. Learn to separate the appreciation of effort and the appreciation of result when you share feedback with the team. Very often we appreciate only when the result is achieved – thereby missing an opportunity.

Team, I want to acknowledge and appreciate the hard work we put in for this deal. At the end of the day, I want each one of us to know that it is this kind of effort – where we work as a team without thinking of individual glory – that will determine where we stand in the long run. And yes, while we lost the deal, we also learnt from it. But I don't want the loss to diminish the effort we put in for the deal.

OR

Team, I want to thank you all for a wonderful effort of pulling off the prototype in a short span of time. We planned, replanned, we worked, reworked, we lost patience, but came back with renewed vigour, we iterated, we sought and got feedback and at the end pulled off a magnificent victory. Thank you, every single one of you, for this fantastic team effort.

As Carol Dweck states, praising the effort rather than outcome applies to our world as well. There are times when the effort has to be recognized as well. However, if you are putting in a lot of effort and there are no results, something else needs to be checked, but the moment you learn to distinguish the effort and result in giving appreciative feedback, you will notice that it is easy to separate effort and result when it needs to be called out. Because between two sets of people who put in the same effort, it is likely that the one who delivers consistently might be rewarded differently.

Myth: There is an ideal ratio for appreciation versus critical feedback? No. There is no ideal ratio.

Try this: Is it possible for you to bring appreciative conversations to about 50% of the total conversations you have with the team? What would it take for you to do that? (It is tough, be warned.)

TLDR: Perhaps the most repeated point in the book. The more you Appreciate your team members the easier it is to have difficult conversations with them.

Start by appreciating your team and team members. Appreciation like all aspects of feedback has to be genuine and specific. Keep CORBS in mind, 7 types of appreciation. Appreciate yourself. You can appreciate your team members, peers and supervisors. There are different aspects of appreciating, ranging from acknowledgement to validation to gratitude. Use them well to develop your range of giving feedback. And leave your recipients with great feedback. So, how about appreciating your team more?

Chapter 10

What about Difficult Conversations?

The Cast:

Vani: The boss

Manoj: Manager

Shalini: Manoj's peer manager who is new

Ashwin, Dheeraj: Manoj's team

Chetan, Sushma: Shalini's team

Shalini finds it difficult to give feedback to Chetan – because she thinks Chetan may respond emotionally.

Replace Shalini and Chetan with any two individuals. As managers and leaders, this is a common situation we face.

A difficult conversation can vary in difficulty – yet all of them give the jitters to the person who has to convey the message.

A difficult conversation can be any of the following:

Differing expectation:

"I expected a higher rating. It is unfair that I have been given a lower rating than I expected."

The receiver has somewhat higher expectations of a feedback performance review discussion, and hence is unwilling to accept whatever feedback is given to him.

Different perception:

"I don't agree with you. My technical skills are far superior to what you are sharing as feedback. You don't understand the complexity."

Difficult conversations at work are mostly about different perceptions primarily caused by insufficient communication and incorrect expectation setting. Such conversations can occur between peers or between managers and reportees. It can be a difference of opinion on the process that needs to be followed or even using the right coding standards. It may be a disagreement on delivery dates or project deliverables. It may also be that the receiver of the feedback simply does not agree on the feedback that the giver is giving – there is a reluctance in receiving feedback (assuming the feedback being given is relevant).

Any form of conversation where the parties may not be in agreement can be termed as a difficult conversation. The giver of feedback is unsure about "how the receiver will take it" hence classifies it as a difficult conversation. And usually, it is the receiver who is labelled "difficult" – someone who is unwilling to receive feedback or has unrealistic expectations or behavioural issues.

The reality is that while there is a low probability that the person has real behavioural issues, there is a tendency to paint all difficult conversations with the same brush. The problem with this framing is that it prevents the real issue from being seen – which is the skill + data gap in being able to accomplish a difficult conversation.

Shalini, "I have exciting news for you, Sushma. You have been asked to join the Belgium team for a year. They think having you there would substantially speed up the delivery of the current feature that you are working on."

Sushma, "I don't want to discuss this at all" (working in Belgium is the worst thing).

Later

Shalini, "I have been offering Sushma a chance to travel abroad, but she just doesn't want to go. She does not even want to bring up the topic. I can't, for the life of me, understand why something like this – which is such a good thing – ticks her off."

Vani, "Have you asked her why?"

Shalini, "Well, usually when it ticks her off, I drop the topic. I have never really explored why that is the case. She is just a difficult person I suppose."

Vani, "Why don't you ask her and see?"

Second Attempt

Shalini, "I know you did not want to discuss the Belgium opportunity, but I want to know a little more about your reluctance."

Sushma, "I don't want to discuss this at all."

Shalini, "I hear you. I am keen to know more, Sushma, as your response is unusual – from what I have seen, it is exciting for anyone."

Sushma, "Oh, this is not exciting at all. On the contrary, it is just not an option for me and I don't want to talk about it."

Shalini, "May I ask you why?"

Sushma, "Well. I can share this if you promise to be non-judgemental."

Shalini, "Sure."

Sushma, "If I bring this up with my spouse, he is sure to be upset. He cannot imagine us living away from his parents. And it leads to many fights at home which I don't have the energy to face."

Shalini, "Oh is it. I had no idea. I was under the impression this is a great opportunity and most people tend to go all out for it."

Sushma, "Well, it is an opportunity, but we have our reasons."

Shalini, "Yes ... and?"

Sushma, "And to be honest, my parents as well, but I may be able to convince my parents that it is for just a year. It will be difficult to convince because his parents are older and need care and he is the only child."

Shalini, "I never realized this was the situation you were dealing with and I always wondered what the issue could be."

Sushma, "Well, this is very difficult for me. I don't know what to do."

Shalini, "Understandably so, thanks for sharing."

What is perceivably an easy conversation could be difficult in a different way that the giver never anticipated it.

Here is another example:

Bill is the head of XYZ Technologies, which is a large customer for Vani and team.

Vani, "You will have to tell Bill that the current numbers won't work in the coming year."

Manoj, "Why?"

Vani, "The board feels that we need to price our services more in tune with the market."

Manoj, "But they have been with us for years – from the time we were a fledgling firm. They will not be happy at all. Also we have signed a 3-year agreement with them. We will have to have a really strong reason to ask for a revision. It is not going to be easy at all."

It could be a conversation where the stakes are high.

Vani: Manoj, your OKRs are showing a gap.

Manoj: Well, this is partly owned by Shalini, but she is not devoting enough resources to get it done.

Shalini: I had no idea that this is partly owned by me – it was never communicated to me.

Manoj: It is on the sheet – all you had to do was to see it.

Shalini: That sheet has 26 OKRs and they all have my name on it and my team is working on them. Nowhere did we say that this is my priority and you need my time.

Behind many difficult conversations is a communication gap.

Chetan: When I joined, I was promised a promotion in 6 months.

Shalini: We don't make such promises when someone joins. Can you tell me who made such a commitment?

Chetan: I asked the recruiter if I can get promoted in 6 months and the recruiter said yes.

Shalini: Chetan, that is not the same thing as a commitment. Theoretically, the recruiter is right, and that does not automatically translate into a commitment that at the end of 6 months you will be promoted. There are various factors.

Chetan: Well, then the recruiter should have shared it that way. This feels like a let-down.

It could be an incorrect expectation setting.

As we move towards the right in the diagram, the skill becomes exponentially more difficult. And this is where true leadership shows up. The ability of a leader to maintain calm while having a difficult conversation and steer the conversation to safe shores is a useful skill. From convincing difficult people to managing bosses, negotiating a budget and taking people along, this is one skill that is handy in all situations.

What makes a difficult conversation more difficult is a lack of skill to handle a difficult conversation, the lack of practice that manifests as a fear, the lack of preparation to have the conversation (the most underrated of all of them) and the unsureness of the feedback to be shared or point of view to be held or contested. Very similar to the fear in giving feedback.

> Sure, some leaders have been historically bad at convincing people. They are known to use a combination of power, authority, charisma and are often quoted and taken as an example in management lore to "be yourself." While there is some probability of becoming a good leader without taking the trouble to develop good conversation skills considering that most of us are not tech barons with high charisma, conversation skill might be a skill worth developing.
>
> [Do keep in mind that mostly when management lore talks of leaders, management lore equates that to founders of highly successful companies.]

Here is what a difficult conversation framework looks like.

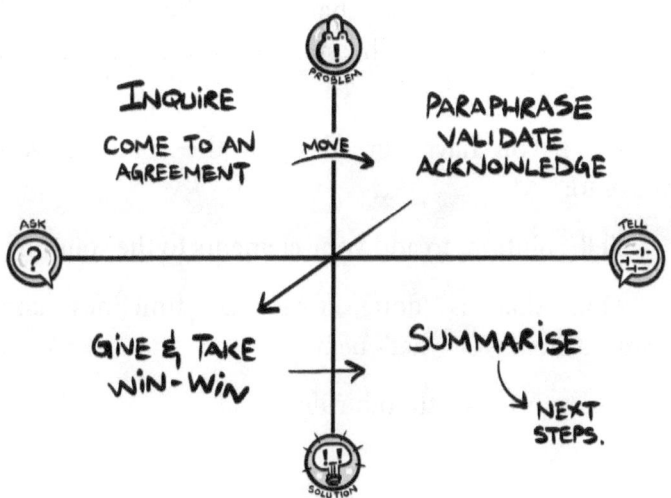

Start at Ask/Problem quadrant. The spirit is that of inquiry and curiosity. Seek to understand.

Start by asking: What do you think, why do you think so, what would you like …

Once you come to a broad agreement, move to the next quadrant. Tell/Problem. Here you will Paraphrase/Summarize your understanding of the problem. You will also validate and acknowledge the other side. And Express yourself in "I think …<state the common understanding of the problem>" This step is crucial because both sides have to agree that a problem exists and agree on the definition of the problem. Most of the time this is the failure point.

Next you move to:

Ask/Solution. Here it is all about breaking the solution: give and take, curiously understanding each other and trying to see what part of the solution will work or won't work. The spirit of this negotiation is win–win.

Once you have agreed upon the solution, you move to:

Tell/Solution, to add your elements to the solution.

One that is done, formalize timelines and commitments for what's next.

Therefore, as a thumb rule

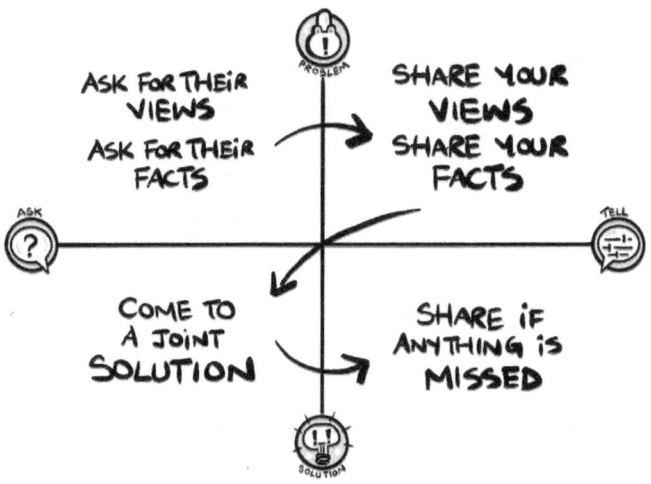

- Ask for their view
- Ask for their facts
- Share (not assert) your facts
- Share you view
- Test, where they stand
- Ask for a solution/resolution
- Share anything that has been left out
- Agree on next steps
- Closure

The framework remains the same. Tackling difficult conversations is all about asking questions, asking clarifying questions, zeroing in on the issues agreed upon and disagreed upon, seeing the other person's perception, listening and resolving.

M: "Bill, we wanted to have a discussion on the possible revision of the contract."

B: "I am sure you are kidding, right?"

M: "No, Bill. I am not kidding. I really want to get into a discussion with you on this and know your views on it."

B: "No, I am not open to this conversation."

M: "Perhaps you could share your views around it."

M: "No obligation to revise the contract, but I do want to factor in your views."

B: "With your current features, this price itself is high for me."

M: "What if we evaluated the features?"

B: "Well, I am willing to look at it."

This is a good start.

If Bill shares facts, that is a good place to be.

If he doesn't, you have to get him to a point where he is willing to share facts. (The degree of difficulty depends on whether he does it in a transparent manner. If Bill resorts to skipping meetings, not answering emails, you have to share feedback about that before you get him to the point where he can share facts with you.)

He has in a way already shared his view – but the difficulty here is that his view has to be changed. Therefore, it is important that you see his view as well.

The idea is to be gentle at each stage, calmly share feedback if Bill crosses the line, but at each stage follow the tenets of the difficult conversation.

The next stage is to come to an agreement that the problem is real, that you need a revision in contract because your current price is too low. (Bill may or may not agree to it. That needs facts. The facts will help Bill see the issue for what it is.)

Since you already have his view, you also want his side of the facts and see what the points of agreement and the points of disagreement from his side are.

Manoj: Bill, I do see that your issue is not with the pricing going up per se, but you want better support in newer features.

Bill: If you can promise the 8 new features in the coming year, that will give us a lead in the market and we can agree to the higher price.

Manoj: We can bake that into the contract and go in for a tiered pricing model. How does that sound?

Bill: We can discuss that when we get there.

[this is one sided]

Manoj: It will help if we can identify a mutually workable pricing model to see things in perspective.

Communication:

Manoj: Fair point, I did not realize that. I should have had a conversation with you.

Shalini: I could have also checked, but I did not.

Manoj: How can we work this through now?

Shalini: Why don't we go over that list and see what can be done?

Manoj: Yes. And to that, let's also identify points of contacts in your team for them.

Mutual acknowledgement of the problem is a good first step to resolve issues.

Promotion:

Shalini: I hear you. I think we need to check if such a commitment is being made to prospects – however vague.

Chetan: I have heard it from a few others as well.

Shalini: Let me take this up.

Chetan: I should have shared this with you at the joining time – I assumed that it was a formal commitment.

Shalini: Chetan, thanks for sharing this with me. I may not be able to do anything in this cycle – but let me see if there is a resolution I can bring about here.

TLDR: The conversation framework can be adapted for difficult conversations. Tackling difficult conversations is all about asking questions, asking clarifying questions, listening empathetically, seeing the other person's perception, zeroing in on the issues agreed upon and disagreed upon and to listening and resolving with a win–win approach. Try using the difficult conversations framework in a feedback/difficult conversation at work.

Chapter 11

Use Questions to get Better at Feedback

If there is one skill to be built by leaders that would encapsulate all of conversation, feedback, coaching and mentoring, it would be this: Asking a good question. Note that is not about asking the right question. Questions open up conversations.

> During my first assignment in the US, our first meeting was with an American who was our client. She asked us how we were planning to complete a particular deliverable. And our lead responded, "Don't worry we will get it done." He simply said, "Don't worry".
>
> The client was upset. They complained to the account manager saying your team is taking things too casually. When the lead got this feedback from the AM, the lead was upset. He told the AM he had reassured the client that they would do what it

> takes to complete the project. But it had not landed well with the client.
>
> The answer the client was expecting was, "We will send you a detailed project plan and a daily status update."
>
> The lead did share a plan the very next day with apologies, never closing the conversation with either the account manager or the client. Instead, he cribbed to his peers about how these Americans went into planning without doing actual work (again, a perception). In a nutshell, a story that encapsulates our approach when it comes to asking clarifying questions and closing conversations.
>
> *A simple question here by the lead would have made the situation very different.*
>
> *"Sure, what would you like from our side?"*
>
> *The client would have replied, "Would you be able to share a plan?"*

How to ask good questions? There are two types of questions, open ended and close ended. Close-ended questions are required to come to agreement or to close a conversation or to zero in on something. Open-ended questions on the other hand are expansive, broaden the understanding and enable us to get a bird's eye view.

What does a question do in a conversation? Simply put, it puts the brakes and slows down thinking. As long as your question makes the other person pause and think, you are on the right track. The key to asking good questions is just one word.

Curiosity.

Ask a curious question. As opposed to, a judgemental question.

What is the difference between a curious question and a judgemental question?

Pranav at a meeting with Manoj says, referring to Atul who is leading the project. Atul may be the project lead, but he is not the technical expert, I am.

Manoj is surprised by this assertion.

Case A: Manoj is curious.

Curious question (in Manoj's head): Well, Pranav is the technical lead indeed, wonder what made him assert his position.

The question Manoj asks: Sure Pranav, wondering what made you say that Atul is not the technical expert.

Case B: Manoj makes a judgement.

Judgemental question (in Manoj's head): What does he think he is, calling out the team leader in a meeting.

The question Manoj asks: Atul is the leader and you are expected to back him up. Why did you make a statement like that in the meeting?

Deepa is going to join your team, says the boss to Shalini. Deepa is the same person who Shalini did not get along with 3 years ago when they were in different roles.

Curious question (in Shalini's head): I wonder why.

The question she asks: Sure, in what role?

Judgemental question (in Shalini's head): I don't think I can work with Deepa given our previous equation. Can this be changed somehow?

The question she asks: Oh, I am not sure I want to be in the same team as Deepa. Do I have a choice?

Situation: Yesterday's software update did not make it to production.

A judgemental question puts the focus on the person and sounds like blaming. For example,

Judgemental Question: Who was in charge? Why can't you get a simple update right?

A curious question puts the focus on the issue and sounds curious.

For example,

Curious question: What was the issue with the patch? Can you share the RCA (root cause analysis)?

A Judgemental question puts the focus on the past and sounds like interrogation/looks only at the problem. For example: This is the second time in the last month this has happened. Who is leading this effort?

A Curious question puts the focus on the future and looks at a solution. For example: Guys, can you get together and come up with a root cause analysis and a mitigation plan for the future?

A Judgemental question puts the focus on the other person. For example: Why do you always make such silly mistakes?

A Curious question brings both parties into focus. For example: What are we missing in these updates that it doesn't pass the testing?

The second type of question is the Clarifying Question. In all my observations as an assessor or facilitator or team member the common thing I see people miss is the clarifying question. Equally curious, but it pushes the pause button on the reactive mind which is waiting for an emotional hijack, and seeks clarity with curiosity. Not all curious questions are clarifying questions, but all clarifying questions are curious questions.

Clarifying questions can be both open and close ended, but in general, follow a divergent–convergent approach. Start with open-ended questions (diverge) and close with close-ended questions (converge).

A good clarifying question could be deeper (why is it important?), curious (tell me more), cause the receiver to pause and think (and?), show possibilities (what would happen if …), open doors (is there anything else?) as the open-ended one. Then you can move to close-ended clarifying questions such as, can you be specific (specific)? Can you think of a solution?

Beware of the close-ended question disguised as a clarifying question. For instance, "What do you think of improving XYZ" is really not a clarifying question as much as it is a leading question. However, "what do you think of XYZ" is a clarifying question.

So, in this situation where Shalini's brain feels threatened <Deepa will be joining our team>, it pauses and asks, "tell me more" or "I am curious" or "And?"

Shalini, "Tell me more."

Vani, "Deepa is looking for a new role and this was the best fit."

S, "Hmm, Any specific reason why this team and this role?"

V, "Well, this is the only role available for her level of experience."

S, "Given that we have had a difficult working relationship before, should I be worried?"

V, "Yes, I am aware of it. And well, that was some time back and I am hoping both of you have grown since then. Plus she will report to you, unlike earlier when you were peers. I would not be worried if I were in your place."

The clarifying question cools you down – makes you calmer and you respond to the situation better. And that is usually not expected by the person on the other side. So, the other person gets a chance to explain her view in a better manner and often clarifies her thinking as well while giving you an invaluable perspective.

TLDR: Tell me more. What else? Is there more to it? What part of it do you disagree with? What do you think? What could be better? What part of this solution are you comfortable/uncomfortable with? Use clarifying questions to diverge as well as converge.

Chapter 12

The Receiver is Equally Afraid

Vani: Why is it so difficult for people to take feedback?

Manoj: Most of the time, people think whatever they are doing is right. Maybe they are subject matter experts and think they don't need feedback?

Shalini: Partly because it is not delivered well?

Vani: While those are good reasons, do think of what happens to the receivers when they receive feedback? Think about how you felt when you received feedback, specifically something you thought went well and received critical feedback on it, for the first time.

Manoj: I remember, I was furious with my manager.

Shalini: I was angry first and then in denial for some time.

Manoj: I also remember some degree of defiance.

Vani: Have you ever thought, what actually happens when you give feedback? It is one thing to say, I want to give feedback, but every so often, the feedback that you give does not land properly. For some reasons unknown to you, the person doesn't take it well. And you wonder why. After all, the feedback was based on CORBS, had facts and evidence at their disposal and was obvious. So, what went wrong? And we label the person, depending on how they react – either as difficult or as sensitive.

Shalini: I for one sure do.

Manoj: I have generally thought feedback was useless after my first experience but now I am learning.

Long back, as a management trainee – one of my peers received critical feedback from his manager. And he did not like a single word of what he heard. He thought the person in question who gave him the feedback did not like him. He felt the feedback was prejudiced. He said, "I was a college topper. I have been doing well everywhere, so this is unbelievable. How is it possible?"

The acronym DERAC explains the stages of thought when one receives feedback.

Denial: It is not me.

Emotion: Why me? Followed by anger, frustration.

Rationalization: Let me think about it.

Acceptance: Assuming the feedback was real, accept the feedback as given.

Change/Continue: Hopefully, the feedback results in real change.

Knowing these stages is important because as a manager/leader one tends to think a feedback is obvious, but it is not so obvious for the receiver.

When the manager is hit by the Denial and Emotional reaction, the manager also has her self-doubt or biases triggered. It can also take the form of DERAC for the manager, because the non-acceptance of the feedback is feedback to the manager.

"Did I not give the feedback well?" or "Will this person make this an issue" or "Was this feedback not right at all" or "This is why he will never improve – waste of my time" or "What an idiot" and thus self-doubts, biases and blame kick in and a manager holds back and does not give feedback the next time around. The D of DERAC is a stage, not an attitude problem.

TLDR: Wait for the feedback to be accepted or challenged as more data is presented. Continue to have conversations being aware of the DERAC stages. Be aware of your own DERAC stages when you receive uncomfortable feedback.

Chapter 13

Making Feedback Work for You

In reading and researching for the book, the strongest reason I got for receiving feedback was from the book, *Thanks for the Feedback*.[15]

The author says,

"The real leverage is creating pull. Creating pull is about mastering the skills required to drive our own learning; it's about how to recognize and manage our resistance, how to engage in feedback conversations with confidence and curiosity, and even when the feedback seems wrong, how to find insight that might help us grow. It's also about how to stand up for who we are and how we see the world, and ask for what we need. It's about how to learn from feedback – yes, even when it is off base, unfair, poorly delivered, and frankly, you're not in the mood.

We like the word "pull" because it highlights a truth often ignored: that the key variable in your growth is not your teacher or your supervisor. It's you. It's well and good to hope for that special mentor or coach (and cherish the ones you come across). But don't put off learning until they arrive. Those exceptional teachers and mentors are rare. Mostly, our lives are populated by everyone else – people who are doing their best but may not know better, who are too busy to give us the time we need, who are difficult themselves, or who are just plain lousy giving feedback or coaching. The majority of our learning is going to have to come from folks like these, so if we're serious about growth and improvement, we have no choice but to get good at learning."[16]

Very often in an individual setting, when you ask for feedback it is likely that you will get

a, superficial feedback

or

b, vague feedback

Once I asked my manager. *"It's been three months in the team. I would like your feedback on my work since the time I took over."*

"All good. All good."

"Ok. Is there something that should change?"

"No, no. Do more of what you are doing."

The feedback was thoroughly useless except for a momentary feel good and I did not realize it at that time. Neither did I realize it another 3 months down the line when I had the same conversation. But 3 months later, I was hit by a long list of things I needed to work on. I was obviously surprised. That's when I realized my mistake in the first two conversations.

What I could have done better in the first conversation was this:

"May I seek specific feedback on 2 things? First: How am I managing the team? Second: How is the quality of my work? I know that these were the two issues on your mind when I took over this role."

And maybe I would have heard this:

"Ah, yes. Let me see. I have been hearing good things from your team in my skip-level meetings and from the stakeholders. But here is what I will do. Let me come back to you in a week and give you an update."

And a week later, I would have heard, "X (one of the key stakeholders) wants the team to be more proactive. He feels you guys are not pulling your weight enough with the sales teams." And that would have alerted me then than what came my way 6 months later.

The vague feedback left me thinking that all was well all along. Therefore, seek specific feedback if you get vague responses. Seek feedback on 1–2 things only.

Sometimes you will hear feedback that is diametrically opposite to what you have heard before.

"K, Can I give you some feedback?"

"Sure."

"K, I think your execution has been weak in the past quarter."

Now K's well-known strong point is his execution ability. What does K do? K can either have an emotional hijack or he can ask a curious question.

"I am curious, tell me more?" says K

"There were several complaints from the clients last few weeks on Project Alpha."

"Yes and they were all issues that we had taken cognisance of given it was a new project. And we closed all of them within SLA and updated the client. Is there something else?"

"No, I think this is it."

Clearly, in this case the manager had generalized feedback over a few specific issues and shared it as a generalized comment to K.

3 months later.

"K, Can I give you some feedback?"

"Sure."

"K, you remember I had mentioned a few execution issues?"

"Yes."

"I think there is more to it. I have been going over the issue log, and I feel, one thing you can work on is to be proactive rather than reactive."

"Sure. Tell me more."

"I see that all issues raised are being closed within the SLA. But there is no reduction in the number of issues. It has been a constant flow for 3 months now."

"Hmmm. I never thought of it that way."

"Can you think about a plan to taper the issues to zero and revert?"

K considers planning as his strength. K cross-checks this with a couple of people he trusts, people who he has worked with in the past and asks them questions on "did you see me work on the project in a reactive manner as opposed to a proactive manner." This gives K a wider view of the feedback and then he can decide how pertinent it is.

Thus, while every feedback need not be acted upon, it is always good to verify it as part of self-growth. By and large, your strengths will remain with you. If you are strong in execution, you will continue to be (assuming other things being equal) strong in execution, but it is always worth a check.

On the other hand, receiving feedback in a group setting is more difficult than in an individual setting.

Once we had taken a proposal to be reviewed by a set of senior managers for an innovation contest. The group was not sure what to expect with our presentation and we ended up getting feedback that was all over the place. The group did not take it well and

- Took it personally
- Got defensive. They defended every piece of feedback with, "What we meant was this ..." or "Not sure you understand ..."
- Came off as combative

Ideally, the group should have said "thank you," collected the feedback and responded later. They could have ignored some of the feedback – and asked clarifying questions. But in that moment, the group was in a state of "emotional hijack," We realized this much later.

I would be remiss here if I did not mention the need to have a "Growth Mindset" in operation while we are in the space of receiving feedback.

Stanford psychologist Carol Dweck synthesized this in her insightful book, *Mindset: The New Psychology of Success* – a philosophy widely known as Growth Mindset.[17]

Dweck, through her research, came up with two mindsets that operate in people.

One, a "fixed mindset" assumes that our character, intelligence and creative ability are static givens which we can't change in any meaningful way, and success is the affirmation of that inherent intelligence, an assessment of how those givens measure up against an equally fixed standard; striving for success and avoiding failure at all costs become a way of maintaining the sense of being smart or skilled. A "growth mindset," on the other hand, thrives on challenge and sees failure not as evidence of unintelligence but as a heartening springboard for growth and for stretching our existing abilities.[18]

Therefore when we receive feedback, it is important to turn on our "Growth Mindset" receptors. That means telling ourselves that this feedback will enable me to grow and stretch my own abilities. And to keep in mind the larger goal as to why that feedback is important. It also means asking good questions so we clearly know what can be made better. And the idea here is to not agree with every bit of feedback, but to hear/collate it in an open and receptive manner.

Therefore as a feedback giver, remember to focus on the effort.

Tip: It is possible that you end up getting conflicting feedback. One person may say your presentation skills are really good and another person might say your presentation skills are really bad. Ask clarifying questions to both parties to begin with. And then use this to check in with one or two trusted individuals/coaches/mentors/peers to zero in the actionable feedback.

Question: As a manager, should I seek feedback from my team?

Yes. This can be at specific junctures – it can be at the time when you have your regular 1:1s with your team members – where you earmark a specific segment to seek feedback. As part of your annual appraisal conversation you can seek feedback from your team. A casual conversation with your team on "how things are going" and "if they have any feedback to share about you" will help you get a dipstick.

It works in the same manner with your peers as well, and specifically when you work together on projects.

Question: Should I seek anonymous feedback from my team?

In my view, if you are keen on building a culture of feedback – avoid anonymous feedback. Teams and organizations are built not by hiding from each other but by giving genuine, honest feedback with the right intent.

Anonymous feedback assumes that only the giver of the feedback has the right intent, but the receiver doesn't – and this fundamentally flies in the face of building a transparent organization culture – even after accounting for hierarchy. After all, most of us are not working for the mafia!

How often should you seek feedback?

3 months is a good interval. Understand expectations at the start of every milestone and seek feedback at the end. Seek feedback on specific issues – it makes it easier for the team/peers to give you the feedback.

And when you do get feedback, acknowledge and act on it.

How to give feedback in a group setting:

Often you find yourself in a situation where you are part of a group that is asked to give feedback. Sometimes it is feedback on a program, a product proposal, a new project, or a demonstration. Group feedback is one of the most dangerous ones for the presenter who is the receiver of the feedback. For one, if the group does not know how to give feedback, it may result in a significant loss of self-esteem for the presenter apart from other collateral damage.

How to seek feedback from a group:

Before the meeting lay the ground rules for how the meeting will be held. Share the objective and the agenda beforehand. Preferably, ask participants to pre-read or share some reading material.

Set expectations on the nature of feedback, the format of the feedback and the number of points under each head.

Remember to ask for specific feedback.

For instance, if the project is in the conceptual stage, ask for conceptual feedback – ask if the conceptual framework presented is in alignment with the organization goal.

If the project is in the execution stage, ask for feedback on various aspects of implementation, such as quality, time, buy-in from key stakeholders, etc.

If the project is about to be closed, ask feedback on ironing out the creases in the project.

If required, have a moderator (preferably someone who is interested in the success of the project) who ensures that all people have a say and that different opinions are given voice to.

Ask clarifying questions.

Do not defend your idea when you are bombarded with feedback – say thank you for the feedback and reflect on it after the event.

How to give feedback in a group

Overall, the method of giving feedback in a group is not very different from any other feedback. It has to be specific, clear, owned and balanced. What is also important is that you speak as you – for instance, use "here is what I feel" and not "Here is what we feel." Always speak for yourself.

Keep the feedback short and succinct and follow CORBS.

Cover only 1 thing at one time. Or maybe 2. Nothing more.

Watch out for what people appreciate and add accordingly. This is often a blind spot and therefore important – with everybody in the group giving templated feedback, there is space to stand out.

Do not use sandwich feedback – keep appreciation and improvements separate.

Avoid piling on the feedback. If one feedback (for example, product configuration) has already been shared – say +1 and move on. Add value by offering a different insight.

It is ok to stay silent as well if you don't have anything substantial and value adding.

Ask what feedback the presenter wants. Sometimes they are clear on the aspects that they want feedback on.

If you are a leadership team and you have your teams making presentations to you for approval or progress, here is a tip.

Try and ensure that group feedback does not become a reason to poke holes into every aspect of the proposal/idea. Offer the presenter methods on how to patch those holes so that there is focus on the solution rather than just have the presenter listen to opinions flying around. Also share a consensus approach/direction so that the presenter is left with solution focus rather than a problem focus.

Or, one of you can set up time with the project owner before the meeting and guide/mentor those nascent projects into a shape that can be shared with the larger leadership team.

Making feedback work for High Performers: High performers who revel in feedback will keep coming to you seeking feedback. They are good at a few things and having learnt that feedback is the way to grow, actively seek feedback. They don't accept appreciation without justification and want to get into the details on what they can do better. Therefore practice giving good actionable feedback to team members – that means observe, collect evidence and share in a way that they are inspired to work on it.

In my experience high performers often get very little feedback for improvement – they are usually better than the average, so managers often fail to see significant scope for improvement and do not give them sufficient feedback to work on. And they end up getting superfluous feedback.

Use feedback to push the team to do better: I had a reportee in my team who was extremely talented. But her first line of solutioning would almost always come to the level of "meets expectations."

One of my methods to challenge her was to review her work and tell her "While this is good, I feel you can do better than this" and share a few specific points.

Unknown to me, this would challenge her inner creative devil and she would come up with something superlative in the next round.

Truth be told, I wasn't doing this knowingly – I genuinely felt her creative potential was left untapped.

I realized the effect of this on her when she shared this with me after I had left the role.

This method works with high performers – however, like in all cases, it is important to be genuine. The challenge should be posed to their strengths, not to their "lesser talents."

When does it not work: I was once assigned to be part of a quality team for a short while. For someone like me who wanted the freedom to create and ideate, putting me in a quality team to review another team's output by going over a 700-row xls or poring over documents and their versions was as interesting as the smell of cooking cabbage. And my manager said, "This is a great challenge for you."

The challenge has to be appealing. Don't ask your team to put in 2 more hours in a working day that is already 12 hours long. If the challenge is appealing, the time will be put in automatically. Notice how we almost always manage to create time to work on what we love?

Once, as a business analysts, we had to make an educational presentation for our President, who was new to the business (as it was for all of us). And the job came to the new team of Business Analysts. The business was new, and it took me a good amount of time to ferret out information. And to organize it in a manner that will appeal to the President. I worked extra hours (and a couple of weekends – the only weekends I ever worked in my long stint with the firm) to get it out of the door. Because my strengths and interests intersected – I was very happy to work on it. Later, when I took on the training role – the President remembered this session we had done for him 6 years ago.

Tap into areas where the strengths and interests of your team members intersect. However, there might be assignments where you need the team to go beyond the strength or interest to deliver something. In that case, explain the situation so that they know what they are getting into, why this has to be done and a timeline, instead of marketing it to be the best thing in their career which it is not. The more authentic you are, the greater trust you can build with your team.

Tip: One of my methods was to identify a peer who had a different strength than I did and go to him to peer review my work. He did the same with me. And over time, we developed a good rapport and would run our work past each other. It worked well for us because we knew that the other was not being judgemental, had the best interests of the organization in mind and would not shy away from giving feedback. And this is something we do even today every now and then when we want a different perspective. Create a network of such people who will give you unbiased feedback. This kind of prework helps you navigate group feedback better.

Try Feedforward: Marshall Goldsmith speaks of a method called Feedforward – this is all about giving tips, suggestions, observations in advance so that all "Feedback" is future oriented.[19]

TLDR: Seeking feedback is a great way to overcome blind spots and finding gaps in skills and areas of improvement. Generally, people love to give feedback (yes!). Use this to seek feedback from senior members to get better at your work. And make feedback work for you.

Chapter 14

Feedback as the Ultimate Leverage for All Competencies

It was the start of a war. A war they tried their best to avert. And when the two armies came face to face, Arjuna, one of the five Pandava brothers, couldn't bring himself to fight. At that crucial moment, his charioteer, Krishna, had what is considered as the greatest conversation on earth, with Arjuna. The entire conversation is known as the Bhagavad Gita[20] and as you go from chapter to chapter, you realize that it is a conversation between two people. A conversation where Arjuna has doubts, seeks clarifications and Krishna talks to him. The conversation has every aspect of a conversation known to humanity – it results in Arjuna realizing his duty to fight and destroy evil.

Krishna was an avatar – a god descended to earth in human form. All he had to do was to wield his divine weapon (the Sudarshana Chakra) and destroy evil. But he used his conversation skills and brought about the realization in Arjuna to do the right thing.

One way of framing this is that if even a God needs good conversation skills, we after all are mere mortals, we surely do.

Another way to see it is that we all face dilemmas – nothing like the dilemma Arjuna faced – but they are our dilemmas. Often they leave us paralyzed and we are unable to take action. And such dilemmas affect our teams and the people we work with. Conversations are the way to resolve these dilemmas.

And why not? Humans communicate primarily by conversation. Of all the species, humans are the ones who can hold conversations in their heads as stories, orders, instructions as memory. Conversations are used to make friends, fall in love, make enemies, convey ideas, go to war or make peace. And whatever we achieved is a result of this ability – without conversation and language it is arguable that we would not have progressed as much as we did.

Conversations are therefore important, more so when you have to get things done. In the olden days, this could be done by barking orders or cracking a whip, but today, the main method is communication and conversation.

When you have to coordinate teams, convince each other or get something done; in peer groups or on leadership tables; whether you are a fledgling startup or a global giant, this ability is the key for every aspect of work life.

This skill is unlikely to diminish in importance. On the contrary, this skill will be all the more important in these days of digital overload and the reduction in human-to-human contact.

Yet, there are many non-conversational feedback mechanisms that humans employ. Avoidance of eye contact, a terse answer, a half smile, a gesture, body language that says, "I am avoiding you." Or in these days of virtual communication, the audio or video mute button, or a message that is not responded to.

As a leader how would you sort out interpersonal issues, conflicts, egos and get teams to work together? What would it take for your leadership table (to begin with) to sort these?

The answer is, conversations, and that too, candid conversations. And it all starts with Feedback. Feedback is the glue to almost everything you do at work.

Why is conversation the foundational/fundamental skill for all leaders (anybody who is manager and above)?

Take a look at your calendar. If you aren't talking in all those meetings, what are you doing? Yes possibly you are listening – and responding.

We analyzed a set of leadership competencies. And we found that conversation is the key aspect in every one of people management competencies.

Do you want your teams to be creative? Unless you can give and receive feedback on ideas, you will be the lone wolf. And how do you take people along? By talking to people.

Are you leading high-performing teams? A large part of your skillset is the ability to have conversations – and I don't mean banter over a coffee. I mean focused conversations. Hard conversations.

Think of team behaviour:

You want the team to develop trust. You have to get the team to talk to each other and work with each other. Conversation is the basis, not values cards strung from ceilings.

You want the team to collaborate. That means sharing common goals, holding each other accountable and getting things done together. Conversation is the basis, not speeches on collaboration.

You want the team to resolve conflict. Conversation is the basis, not long email threads with the world on CC.

You want to move the manager from directing to coaching. Good luck doing that without a series of conversations. Conversation is the basis.

You want the team to pull each other up, you want transparency, you want a culture of "make it happen." Great partnerships are based on good feedback. Again, it boils down to Conversations.

Try some more competencies!

Stakeholder management?

Influencing skills?

Executive Presence?

Focused conversations again!

And the first step towards building good conversation skills is to build your skills in giving and receiving feedback.

Conversation is a skill to be practiced and worked on. None of us are born with it. It takes conscious practice to have a conversation. Look at families – very few families have direct conversations where emotions are not runaway horses. Look at successful marriages. The key is candid conversations. We are not taught this skill in schools. We are not taught this skill in universities or colleges or B-schools. Thus we land fairly unprepared for conversations at work or at life.

And the first hint of a tough conversation triggers our emotion. This is not to say that emotions are bad or unimportant, but in a professional set up, runaway emotions are the enemies of clear conversations.

What is the magic of Direct Conversations?

Direct Conversations reduce friction between colleagues, smoothen team performance and speed up leadership teams to take decisions.

Every conversation that is not had and is passed to the watercooler or results in passive aggressive responses is an additional layer of friction on one's team that hands over yet another sliver of the market to competition. It might sound sensational, but teams that can discuss issues openly and candidly do outrace teams that can't.

Therefore as a leader, it is important to practice one's conversation skills across the conversation continuum.

As you move higher up, the more you need to be willing to receive feedback and the more positive feedback you give (appreciative), the easier it is to give feedback. The more you give feedback, the easier it is to build transparency between intent and action. The key is to be genuine and show that you have the best interest of the team and in moving forward on solutions and not to achieve that fleeting sense of superiority.

Finding your Style

Shalini: "There are situations where I feel Manoj handles certain people better and I don't. And yet, I am not sure I can do it his way."

Vani: "Sometime back, a friend of mine had a problem. 'Two team members of mine are constantly at loggerheads,' she told me over the phone. And me being me, I gave her advice. 'If I were you, I would call both of them into a room; explain to them that their constant bickering was preventing us from taking the right decisions and that I need the two of them to decide what is the way forward in the next one hour...' She did exactly that."

Shalini: "Hmmm …"

Vani: "The next day, she called me and said, 'One of the guys has not turned up today and the second guy is upset and my decision has not moved forward. Any idea what could have gone wrong?'"

Shalini: "Not understanding the situation correctly perhaps?"

Vani: "Perhaps. But more importantly, this method was not her style. Her style, like yours, was a taking people along style – a way where she individually met the team members, addressed their concerns and made them understand. It was a time consuming way, but it was her way. She was also not someone who directly confronted her team on anything – so after she implemented the first step of my advice, she did not know what to do. That's when it struck me, right or wrong, this was her style. So you have to take into account your style. You will have to confront, have direct conversations on issues, but you also need to evolve your style as you do so."

Shalini: "Sounds like hard work."

Vani: "A little awareness while you engage in conversations. Watch what works. Watch what doesn't. And you will get closer and closer to your style each time."

Shalini: "But can I change my style?"

Vani: "If you mean, by change, learn different ways – yes, but you will usually tend to have one style which you are partial towards."

The idea of having feedback frameworks and guidelines is not to turn you into automatons. There is an element of style in it.

Our feedback style usually comes from our strengths. For someone who is a good strategic thinker, her feedback observations will come from her strategic lens. For someone who has an eye for detail, her feedback will be based on a lack of detail. What is important here is to ensure that one does not give feedback only through the lens of what one is good at, but also look at other aspects that may be a blind spot for the receiver.

And remember to acknowledge what has gone well (which might be a blind spot for the feedback giver).

TLDR: Feedback is that one thing that is a stepping stone to many larger conversations and conversation skills. We believe that is the glue that holds all competencies together and the critical method to building your expertise in conversation skills.

Rounding off

As you increase the quantity and quality of feedback to your team, you will see the following changes occur:

- The team thinks more rather than coming to you with problems
- The team is more relaxed with more transparent conversations
- The team is comfortable bringing up uncomfortable issues
- They feel appreciated and hence are amenable to take in feedback
- The overall quality of work goes up

And when they are asked, "Your manager has called you, what goes on in your mind?" their response will be, "I don't know. I am curious." And that's when you know the change is real.

Feedback Decoded

(These are some of the questions people have in my workshops which usually go unanswered in books. I have separated this into two segments – Myths and Questions)

Myth: Sandwich feedback is a method

Short answer: No. The Sandwich feedback model goes back a few decades. The basic premise of this model is that when you give feedback, start by saying something good, follow that up with the bad news and then wrap it with good news again. Like a sandwich – the bad vegetables lie between two good slices of buttered bread.

Subsequent empirical evidence[21] shows that this is the worst method to give feedback. When you start with the good, they are waiting for the bad. When you give feedback about the bad, they hear you, but by now your good comment has been discounted and the last good – well, nobody heard what you wanted to say. And in all likelihood, the sandwiched vegetable has also been discounted.

Also in this process, you are being insincere as a manager and not transparent enough. Plus likely you had to search for two fake bread pieces in order to sandwich the real vegetables.

New evidence (especially as more millennials and Gen Z's come to the workforce) suggests, give direct feedback. And establish a transparent trusted relationship with your team.

Myth: Direct Feedback is aggression

Managers do not give direct feedback because somehow in their minds, direct feedback has been equated with aggression. Direct feedback is not shouting at your team members or insulting them or their parents or slamming the desk with the fist or waving files in their face. Direct feedback is all about saying what you mean and meaning what you say in a quiet, composed tone. Being aggressive during feedback conversations is for people who can't separate their emotions from the message that is to be given.

Often, aggression is misdirected. Imagine that you shout at someone for shoddy work (yes, even shoddy work). In anger, what are the chances that you will focus on the work and not on the person? And even if you did, what are the chances that the person who is receiving your feedback takes it personally? (very high I presume; try role playing it sometime on the receiving end).

Is it wrong to get angry? No. As long you can carefully control and channel the anger.

Myth: My team members will feel bad if I give direct feedback.

Your team will appreciate it if you give them direct feedback – as long as your feedback is based on evidence, follows CORBS and there is a strong element of support in it (as opposed to blame). Yes, even after all this it is possible that the person might feel bad and get defensive. But if you don't give feedback, you are doing a disservice to the person. So, even if the person feels a little bad – it is worth the risk because they will realize you have their best intent in mind as you continue those conversations.

Myth: Productivity will be affected if I give any feedback that surprises them.

That is like saying that I won't change the punctured tyre or let it run on a patch till I reach the destination. It won't work beyond a point. The person and team will never rise above the current level of productivity and the team will be stuck at a level of mediocrity or fall into familiar traps.

Myth: I don't have time to give feedback.

Yes, it is possible that you don't have time to give feedback once in a while when the platform is burning. But surely you don't work on a burning platform day in and day out? Yet the most common thing that gets postponed during a busy week is the 1:1 conversation. But what it means is not actually a lack of time – it is lack of priority. Somehow in the world of activity and busyness there is no time to give feedback to employees.

Myth: We are all working well without feedback anyway.

Actually, that is not the myth. The myth is that day-to-day work is feedback – so why bother. Because it is not. Day-to-day work rarely results in actionable feedback beyond the immediate task at hand. It may be about how to do something or how not to do something, but at the end of the day, the person goes back with very little reflection or thought. That feedback is mechanical. So, while we may think people are getting feedback, they are not. Feedback has to be explicitly given.

Myth: There is nothing personal about it. People should not get emotional.

As Vito Corleone, the fictional character in Mario Puzo's novel, *The Godfather*, says, "It is all personal, every bit of business." And feedback is personal. You may not like it, you may not want others to take it personally, but we are human beings who are basically an ego wrapped in a body. So, yes, assume, it will be taken personally and work on building trust to be able to give all types of feedback.

Myth: If I Step in so much, I will be perceived as a micromanager.

Your objective is to be a fair manager, understand the strengths and weaknesses of the team members, the collective strength of the team and share both positive and critical feedback with the team members. Doing this in a professional manner will build a better relationship with your team. Micromanagers do not step in. Micromanagers do not give space to their teams to think. They want everything done exactly as they say. Step in is about stepping in at opportune moments and sharing authentic feedback.

Question: I can Step in, what if the person becomes emotional?

Emotions are normal – your job is to provide a safe space for the person to express and share your feedback. If you did have a heated exchange, return to the conversation when things have cooled down and clarify.

Question: I have "told" them so many times, yet nothing changes!

Just telling your team to do "something" doesn't work. It is important for the team to see that these are their goals. Unless they feel like they own it, things won't change. Secondly and more importantly, following up on a regular basis is equally important.

Question: How much to follow up?

Once you share feedback, you also have to work with your team members to enable them to work through the feedback and take corrective steps. As Lou Gerstner says in *Making the Elephant Dance*, "People respect what you inspect." Regular follow-ups are a feature of successful change.

Question: I heard a rumour about a team member. Should I give feedback to the team member?

Don't respond to rumours. And definitely do not give feedback on rumours.

Question: What do I do when my peers/superiors give me feedback on my team members?

Ask them for specific examples. Ask them to email and share it with you. Let them know that you will be sharing this feedback with your team member. If they are not willing to do that, hear it out and decide if you want to share it with your team member.

Question: What if I am upset/disappointed with my team?

Share what you feel with the team. It is ok to be vulnerable and share your feelings with the team [on team-related issues].

Question: I am a new manager. How do I go about building a culture of feedback?

Set expectations that you will work towards building a culture of feedback. And let them know that they will receive feedback. And that you are open and willing to receive feedback as well. Once you set these expectations, follow through with your actions.

Question: What should my tone of voice be while I give feedback?

Feedback is an empathetic conversation where both feedback giver and receiver exchange notes on a specific behaviour with evidence. At the end of the conversation, the two parties agree on the feedback and the way forward.

There is no slamming of the desk, walking out of the door in a huff, no flying objects, no slow-motion recording of bullets flying around. It is a professional conversation with the evidence laid out for both parties to discuss.

No personal attacks – but "you are like this only/always" or "you guys will never learn." Do that and you can see your trust levels drop like a stone in water. Yes, you may have seen people do this – get work done by insulting their teams – but experience suggests you can get a lot more done by winning their trust.

Question: How brief should the feedback be?

Keep the feedback brief. Nobody can handle more than 2–3 issues. And once you have identified the issue, cut to the chase, share evidence – all under 10 minutes.

Question: When do I stop giving feedback?

The question to ask is, "Does <the behaviour> have an impact?" If not, you need not give feedback. If you have a doubt, then there is no impact.

E.g.: For instance, in a presentation, you may be tempted to comment on something cosmetic. Refrain, if it has no bearing on the outcome or their personal development.

However, you may want to share it as an observation – not feedback – and make the difference explicit. Do seek permission before you do so (May I share an observation?).

Some other points worth considering are discussed below:

As a manager, I made a mistake

If you have made a mistake as a manager, it is good to share it with your team. By sharing you build trust, because you are being authentic and sharing your vulnerability at the same time. You are also demonstrating a growth mindset by admitting your mistake and learning from it. And likely the team will role model this behaviour.

Balance in CORBS

Find the silver lining in the cloud and the cloud in the silver lining. What this means especially when the going is good, managers avoid looking at what can be better and when things go wrong, we often miss what is working. Train yourself to spot nuances that you can share with your team. And vice versa, when things don't go as initially expected, try and see what is working well and share it. The purpose is to learn; by doing it your team and organization learn. The method, is to observe better and stay close to the work. Also check with stakeholders for feedback and share that with the team.

Be Honest

Be honest in calling out gaps in performance. Conversations have to be direct, with evidence, leaving both the giver and the receiver with no room for doubt. That means, regardless of whether performance goes up or dips, conversations don't stop – they continue – and work towards making performance better.

Praise well

Watch your language while praising. Generally, managers tend to go overboard while praising – using superlative language or extolling someone's virtues, or using generalized terms while appreciating. Learn to be specific while appreciating someone.

Tough love

One of the leaders I admire practices what he calls "tough love." He listens, he is empathetic, asks them for issues and works in the background to resolve those issues so the team can function. But at the end of the day, the team is held accountable for their deliverables and appropriate feedback is given. And the team usually delivers far more – simply because he spends time establishing trust.

Giving feedback to a senior (this one encompasses all three pre-feedback challenges – Fear, Framing and Consequence)

Ultimately, it is a judgement call as to whether you will actually share the feedback, but the method remains the same. The SBI model with the permission is the best method in my view. And you can add "Here is what I felt about it."

Write down feedback before you share it

Writing helps organize your thoughts and keeps you focused in case you get thrown off track (this happens more than you realize). When you write, note down full sentences. Analyze possible responses and prepare yourself for multiple types of responses.

Detailed Examples

Sandwich Feedback #Fail

I took over a new team from a manager. And I was informed that P had been suitably informed that she is going to be put in a performance plan due to her inadequate performance over the last 3 quarters. And in the due course of setting up 1:1s with all team members, I met P.

After the usual pleasantries, I began, "S has told me that he has shared feedback with you." Can you please tell me what he has shared?

After a long story P came to the crux of the feedback, "S told me there were 3 things I had to improve and 2 things I was really good at. So that means plus 2 and minus 3 so I have to improve on 1 thing and once I improve on that one thing, I will be sent onsite (abroad) on assignment."

In the mind of the manager, P was supposed to be put on a performance improvement plan (PIP). In the mind of the employee, S had told her that with 1 thing to improve she was on the cusp of an onsite assignment.

Holding back from giving feedback

B was a member of my team. "B has performance issues." "B is aggressive at times," and "It is very difficult to get any work done out of B." These were the statements I heard as I joined as B's manager.

I found all of this to be true during my interactions with B and I heard the same from other team members too over the following 3 months. So why wasn't this feedback given to B?

Turned out that B knew the Chief of the company. And B would often have direct meetings with the Chief. And the fear in his previous manager's mind was, if the Chief asked him about the feedback given to B, what would he say? And to top it the Chief and the HR Head were big pals – this had apparently put the manager in a spot. and for years, he had held back from sharing strong feedback with B.

And it was not just his manager; earlier predecessors too had shied away from calling a spade a spade. In return B was shunted from team to team until no manager was ready to have him on the team.

So, when I got the chance, we spoke. *B said how frustrated he was with the team and the group and said, "I just wish I was given direct feedback. I can take it. But I am not given any feedback."*

I shared my thoughts with him. I said, I am new to this group, but here is what I see around you. I see that you are frustrated, looking for opportunities, yet nobody is willing to engage with you. What does this point to?

"Well, yes, I did make some mistakes early on and was a difficult person to work, thanks to many personal issues that spilled over at work. But that is past and it looks like I am paying for those sins."

"That is a fair assessment. What do you think you can do?"

"Let me think," he said.

In two weeks he quit the company and went on to have a successful career. And when he quit, the Chief, a thorough professional, did not call anybody or give a dressing down. It thus turned out that it was fear coming in the way of sharing feedback.

Staying focused in a difficult conversation

M was deemed to be an aggressive character, prone to writing sarcastic, angry emails. He was said to be a difficult person to give feedback to. And according to two predecessors, giving him feedback was impossible since he turned around and gave feedback to them instead of listening. With an imposing personality and equal articulation, he was impossible to manage – this was his reputation.

My first altercation was on something that was my mistake. I admitted it and moved forward. But then his behaviour did not change. Every behaviour was escalated as FYI to my boss, so she knew what was going on. Soon, he asked for a tripartite meeting seeking resolution to constant "conflict." In that conversation, I asked my boss to stay quiet and intervene only when I asked her to.

As the conversation went on, M went down the offensive path. Then, as is wont with such conversations, an attempt was made to widen the net, or obfuscate the issue or digress into something entirely unconnected. I did not get distracted. My only objective was to keep M on track to the conversation at hand. Only on the present topic. Nothing else. No arguments on whether he had done a great job for the company. No argument on whether he was good in execution. No argument on his skills. The only point of discussion was the specific behaviour change.

After a nerve wracking 30 minutes of back and forth, M agreed that the tone in the mail was a mistake and he would make amends.

Now what helped me get this right, more than anything else, is the preparation. I wrote down all possible directions that the conversation may take. The notes helped me stay the course and not be distracted by emotional triggers.

If you thought this was the end, it was not.

People revert to their old behaviour sooner. And M also demonstrated the same.

The key is that every time that behaviour is demonstrated, as a manager, one could sit for a 30 minute 1:1 and have a genuine conversation. It took me 6 months and we began to see glimpses of progress and trust. It took a lot of empathetic conversations to traverse this course and effort from both sides to make it happen. So, do not hold back and step in at every opportunity.

Persisting through conversations

J was another reportee of mine. Extremely high performing, he knew his subject matter very well; he knew how to manage the team and all his stakeholders were extremely pleased. His issue was that he did not want anyone to show him his blind spots. In his mind, he was the best performing employee and he knew more than anybody else. He was very clear.

Through multiple 1:1s, every conversation would be dragged and veered to how he was the victim and how the organization hated him and how maybe people around him saw him as a threat and how he was disrespected and how he was just ready to quit the job. Thus showing the mirror failed.

Finally, in another tripartite meeting, he did the same thing to my boss in my presence. And my boss was trapped as well in this quagmire. And at that point, I had the benefit of being an observer, so I asked him, *"Can you reflect on what you said in this conversation?"*

He was about to go back into his own treadmill of a story and I had to resort to "Tell."

I said, *"J, there are two possibilities here. One that you are right and everybody else who is giving you some sort of feedback is wrong – and that means everybody. The second possibility is?"*

He dithered, looked at the ceiling. And asked, *"That I have an incorrect perception?"*

"Hmm. And?"

"And maybe there is some element of truth in what many people are communicating about me."

"And what might that be?"

"My aggression, my inability to work with peers, my inability to take people along."

"Is it possible that these are things worth reflecting on?"

"Hmmm."

"So, just reflect on the last conversation – you practically mentioned that both me and M – sitting in front of you – are wrong. And we being your managers, we have your best interest in mind. My fear is that as you progress in your career, these blind spots will come in the way of your growth."

"Hmmm."

"Is that worth reflecting on?"

"Yes."

A day later, he came back and said, *"Can we discuss a plan to work on my blind spots?"*

"Sure. What do you want from me?"

"I want you to give me immediate feedback whenever you spot something."

"Sure. That's a deal."

[Conversation shortened to make it brief. This was a 3-month journey of ups and downs.]

Bonus – On Written Feedback

I don't recall how my first few appraisal cycles went. Not in terms of whether I performed or not, but in terms of the actual event of the performance conversation. They were all cursory and I thought that was how it was meant to be.

Until one of my managers took me through a performance conversation that changed my view.

As the conversation started, he asked me about my year. And I shared my view. He followed it by reading from a sheet of paper. He shared an incredible level of detail about my job, the way I had gone about it, what worked well and what could be better.

The way the feedback was documented and written caught my eye. My high points were well documented, my strengths were captured well and the critical feedback on where I needed to improve upon were captured with clear evidence as well. There wasn't much to argue – though for the record, I tried.

He then passed on the sheet of paper to me and asked me to read it at length and come back with feedback. I read the sheet a few times – and in that, what struck me were two things. One that the manager truly cared about me as an employee because he had spent time documenting this. The second thing was that by sharing this feedback, he had done me good and shown me a clear path for the promotion by working on the specific feedback. And a lot of the feedback was a blind spot for me.

For instance, I was not great with details and as a Business Analyst, that can be a disaster. But he had paired me with someone who was so logical in his thought process that we never missed a beat. On the other hand, I was able to think both strategically and out of the box, which was an area of improvement for my "buddy." This was just an example, but in the manner in which this was laid out, I was able to see a lot of things for myself. I had the printout with me for a while after that.

Until then, I had not seen any written performance appraisal. Most of my appraisals started with me writing long tomes of my work – like everybody else. Typical performance appraisals start with the goal and a self-appraisal of how you have performed your work. That's where we each write how much of a role we played in rescuing the project – which, with sufficient English, might have qualified for an entry in a creative writing contest or a film script. And the manager responds with a "Agree," "Disagree" or "NA," almost like they choose to write something from a predetermined drop down.

I am sure you would have experienced this at some point or other. A lot of written performance appraisals are ineffective and don't do justice to the employee's efforts. For one, the leaders do not hold it as a sacrosanct process at all – while it surely deserves to be one. Over time, employees do not take the documentation seriously, with replies like agree/disagree/NA and, the sanctity of the appraisal process is lost. The employee thinks, what's the point of writing out in such detail? It will hardly be read. Or it will be responded to with a single word. And at any rate, only that rating or the salary or the promotion matters.

Few years later, I took over a new team. And I went over their performance appraisals in the system. I noticed that year on year, they were exactly the same. They were copy pasted from one appraisal cycle to the other.

The second thing I noticed was vague statements: B's Communication skills need to improve; C needs to be more assertive. Or with definitive statements offered without any evidence: B is a go getter; R is creative.

On both ends of the spectrum, the statements are hardly statements that could be acted upon or made good use of by the employee.

What is it about writing a good performance appraisal that makes it so worthwhile? For one, it shows the employee you care sufficiently enough. Care enough to spend time writing out a detailed appraisal. When you go into detail, writing about the work they did or bring out things they did well, it makes the appraisal worth it for both employee and manager. And you have to have that level of connect with the work to be able to do that as a manager.

And hence this chapter, because this is hardly written about.

So, how to write a good appraisal?

Hygiene level:

- Do not copy paste from one employee to another.
- Do not respond only to what the employee has written in their self-appraisal.
- Approved, Agree, Disagree and NA are not any component of written feedback.
- Write in complete sentences.
- Use the name of the employee

Moderate level:

- Write about what you saw the employee do – skills, competencies, values. Kumar is a business analyst. His main role is to ensure that we get business requirements on time for our projects.
- Call out high points – Kumar has ensured that all business requirements are diligently captured for all of last quarter projects.

- Use evidence as much as possible – In projects where Kumar was our Lead Business Analyst our overall testing rate has been at 98%.

- Call out patterns. His ability to consistently deliver on requirements (even though we are working on ever new areas of business) is an asset for the team.

- Call out strengths. Kumar is a fast learner. He can understand the fundamentals of a new domain fairly quickly. With an eye for detail and speed of work, it enables the team to turn around solutions within SLA.

- Avoid superlatives like these – Kumar is the best. Kumar is exemplary. Kumar has shown stellar dedication.

Advanced skills:

- Call out nuanced areas of improvement: Kumar can work on data analysis. This is a new skill that is becoming very necessary in his line of work.

- Call out skills that are nascent, but can take the employee a long distance: Kumar has the ability to write white papers – something he has done last year as co-author. This is something he can get better at.

- Give a well-rounded summary. Kumar has been part of this team for 2 years now. He has a keen eye for detail, brings a sense of urgency, has a fast turnaround and gets along with the team.

The rest of the team likes to work with Kumar. The 3 projects he handled in the last quarter all had slightly different challenging aspects – but he managed to negotiate a steep learning curve – and delivered them on time. [Tip – use your company values to anchor conversations – both written and verbal and back it up with evidence.]

- Kumar would do well to polish his formal communication skills – that is one aspect he can work on. He can learn data science – we have opportunities to learn in the company.

- Overall, Kumar has been an asset to the team and I wish him all the best for the coming quarter.

But at heart, it is important that you care. And you will notice this as you write – the ones you care about – you will have more information and for the rest it tapers off. So that means you need to spend more time understanding their work and giving them incisive feedback. And on the other hand, if you are tempted to give a "just continue to do what you're doing" for your high performers, pause. Your high performers deserve better.

A well-written appraisal is a powerful tool in driving engagement and motivating your team. Use it well – simply because the rest of the market does not care enough or know enough of the goodness of this tool.

Tip: Note taking is a strength when you have to give feedback in any context. Write, write, write so that you can share a really good, detailed feedback.

So, bringing real behaviour change through feedback is possible – it requires significant, persistent effort by the manager. Having accomplished this a few times, I would say that it is possible, but as a manager you have to be invested in the person's growth. And that is a good question to ask yourself. As a manager, are you really vested in that person's growth? And in that case are you willing to engage in empathetic, continuous, consistent feedback? And look at other causes. For instance, performance issues at early career stages are often due to being assigned an incorrect role (apt for their skillset), incorrect expectations or in a minority of cases, an attitude problem.

Appendix

Apart from the SBI model for giving feedback there are several others. The most well known is the STAR model by Development Dimensions International (DDI). It's based on 3 simple components:

ST: Situation/Task – Explain the situation or task that you are referring to so others understand the context.

A: Action – Give details about what the person concerned did to handle the situation.

R: Result – Describe what was achieved by the action and why it was effective.

Whether structuring an interview or feedback, the STAR model is a powerful tool.

To guide development in those learning moments, DDI also created the STAR/AR method:

ST: Situation/Task – Explain the situation or task.

A: Action – Give details about what the person concerned did to handle the situation.

R: Result – Describe the consequences, and why the action was ineffective.

A: Alternative action – Discuss what could have been done differently.

R: Alternative Result – Share how the different action could have produced a better result.

With the STAR/AR format, you can give feedback that turns mistakes into positive lessons.

Other feedback models:

BEEF (Behaviour, Example, Effect, Future)

AID (Action, Impact, Development or Desired Behaviour)

EEC (Evidence-Effect-Change)

BIFF model (Behaviour, Impact, Future, Feelings) adds an additional step at the end to gauge how the individual feels after receiving the feedback.

All these models are similar to SBI (Situation, Behaviour, Impact model) in structure. The three phases are setting context, specific behaviour and subsequent Impact.

All these frameworks can be used in an "Ask" or in a "Tell" mode.

You can start by asking people their thoughts about the Situation, Behaviour or Impact. And switch to Tell in case something has to be added.

How do people typically listen: David Rocks sums it up in *Quiet Leadership*:

- Listening for opportunities to sound intelligent
- Listening for a chance to seem funny
- Listening for how you can sound important
- Listening to get information you want
- Listening to external distractions such as other noises, music, etc.
- Listening for what's going on with the other person
- Listening to your own thoughts, and not listening at all
- Listening to see how you can help
- Listening to understand the problem
- Listening for how you can benefit

[This is a valuable exercise in self-awareness. Next time you listen to someone, see which of these approaches you think of. For my part, I am usually thinking of ways to solve the problem and end the conversation and am sometimes thinking how I can sound intelligent. Mea culpa] [David Rock, *Quiet Leadership*]

Get that appraisal conversation right:

Why is the performance conversation such a nightmare? Why do companies go into overdrive just before the performance management cycle and train everybody in performance appraisal conversations?

And why is it that, even after these performance management feedback sessions and workshops, there is no real change?

Let look at this in detail:

What does an employee want as part of their Performance Appraisal?

- How am I doing?
- Manager cares about me
- Manager has an insight about my work
- My work is appreciated
- I get specific areas of feedback – good and bad
- My manager is fair
- My work and contribution is valued
- My work is evaluated objectively
- My role is important to the team/company
- My manager has spent time in the review – done homework
- My feedback is unique – not templated

What does the manager want out of a Performance Appraisal with her team member?

- An idea of the employee's state of mind
- Know that employees have a long-term relationship with the company

- Know if is one adding value as a manager
- Employees feel they work with a good manager, good team
- The team is able to explore their strengths fully
- They see a career here – not just a job
- They go back convinced about the rating and rewards – even if not 100% happy

The above expectations seem reasonable enough, so why are performance conversations dreaded on both sides?

Through the many workshops, what I have gathered is that the key issue in Performance Conversations is not the actual grade or the salary hike that people get, but it is that they are surprised (negatively). It is a shock, real or perceived. They expect a promotion or a hike and don't get it.

However, if the expectation has been rightly set through continuous conversation – with meaningful and actionable feedback backed by evidence, the performance appraisal conversation is no longer a surprise.

And why does that not happen? The short answer is that, when you ask what is the most common meeting that gets cancelled – the answer almost always is "Manager-Reportee 1:1." So, the time reserved for catch ups keeps getting postponed. Or ends up in discussion of trivial issues.

Companies, Teams and Managers that ensure the cadence of the 1:1s are relatively successful in managing the performance appraisal season.

The linkage between missed 1:1s and good performance conversations is simply this – continuous conversations. And that ensures that the performance appraisal is not a surprise for the receiver. And the subsequent reaction is not a surprise for the appraising manager.

Tip: If everything has been discussed throughout 1:1s with continuous feedback on the work done, there is no negative surprise at the Appraisal. Then the appraisal conversation is a wrap of the last 6 months with a special emphasis on career direction, way forward and it becomes a forward-looking conversation as opposed to a backward looking one

And as companies move away from Performance Ratings continuous conversations has become the norm. Yet, from what I hear, this is what comes in the way of making the rating less performance management successful – the lack of continuous conversations.

Companies that have made the 1:1 ingrained into their culture and ensured rich meaningful conversations have made this transition largely smoothly.

So, how to have that conversation?

Start with Asking: "How was the performance?"

Broadly Agree, Thank and move to Tell to add your observations, inputs, value additions. It is important to share your view here.

Move to Solution. Start with Asking: "What could you do better?"

Broadly Agree, Thank and move to Tell to add your observations, inputs, value additions. Again, sharing your view is important.

Agree and close. Seek next steps soon.

Note: The success of an appraisal is determined by the number of conversations you have before the appraisal – the more the number of conversations, the greater your chance of a successful appraisal. The earlier conversations eliminate any chances of a nasty surprise at the appraisal – since everything has been discussed by and large and the contours of the feedback are known.

Notes and References

Because of the very nature of the book, some of my statements are anecdotal rather than researched. I have taken care to state which of these are anecdotal so that it is not perceived as a blanket statement.

1. https://www.hofstede-insights.com/country-comparison/india/#:~:text=India%2C%20with%20a%20rather%20intermediate,in%2Dgroup(s). India scores high on this (Power Distance) dimension, 77, indicating an appreciation for hierarchy and a top-down structure in society and organizations. Communication is top down and directive in its style and often feedback which is negative is never offered up the ladder.

2. https://www.hofstede-insights.com/country-comparison/india/#:~:text=India%2C%20with%20a%20rather%20intermediate,in%2Dgroup(s). India, with a rather intermediate score of 48, is a society with both collectivistic and individualist traits. The collectivist side means that there is a high preference for belonging to a larger social framework in which individuals

are expected to act in accordance to the greater good of one's defined in-group(s).

3. https://www.ccl.org/articles/leading-effectively-articles/closing-the-gap-between-intent-and-impact/#:~:text=The%20Situation%2DBehavior%2DImpact%20method,holding%20talent%20conversations%20with%20employees.

4. https://news.gallup.com/businessjournal/124214/driving-engagement-focusing-strengths.aspx

5. I could not find a reference for the origin of CORBS, but I found this: https://rapidbi.com/cobs-or-corbs-feedback-model-for-performance-management/#:~:text=History%20of%20CORBS%20feedback%20model,into%20wider%20general%20management%20training. The earliest reference I have been able to find for this is from by Peter Hawkins and Robin Shohet in their book *Supervision in the Helping Professions* (2000). The model appears to have developed in the world of teaching medicine, and in 2012 moved into wider general management training

6. *Indian Managers and Organizations*, Ashok Malhotra, p. 125, Routledge, 2019.

7. https://www.hofstede-insights.com/country-comparison/india/#:~:text=India%2C%20with%20a%20rather%20intermediate,in%2Dgroup(s). India, with a rather intermediate score of 48, is a society with both collectivistic and Individualist

traits. The collectivist side means that there is a high preference for belonging to a larger social framework in which individuals are expected to act in accordance to the greater good of one's defined in-group(s).

8. *Thanks for the Feedback*, Viking, 2014, Douglas Stone and Sheila Heen.

9. *The Coaching Habit*, Michael Bungay Stanier, Lake Book Manufacturing, 2016.

10. *Quiet Leadership*, David Rock 2006 Harper Collins.

11. *Quiet Leadership*, David Rock 2006 Harper Collins.

12. http://www.ericberne.com/transactional-analysis

13. http://www.sarahbedrick.com/6-leadership-methods-for-accentuating-the-positive-not-focusing-on-the-negative/

14. *Radical Candor*, Kim Scott, Macmillan 2017.

15. *Thanks for the Feedback*, Douglas Stone and Sheila Heen, Viking, 2014.

16. *Feedforward*, Marshall Goldsmith, Writers of the Round Table, 2012.

17. *Mindset: The New Psychology of Success,* Carol Dweck, Ballantine Books, 2007.

18. *Mindset: The New Psychology of Success,* Carol Dweck, Ballantine Books, 2007.

19. *Feedforward*, Marshall Goldsmith, Writers of the Round Table, 2012.

20. Bhagavad Gita

21. https://hbr.org/2013/04/the-sandwich-approach-undermin#:~:text=If%20you%20give%20a%20feedback,sandwich%20approach%20provides%20balanced%20feedback.

www.ingramcontent.com/pod-product-compliance
Lightning Source LLC
Chambersburg PA
CBHW020901180526
45163CB00007B/2591